Flannery O'Connor

Flannery O'Connor

A Girl Who Knew Her Own Mind

Mary Carpenter

The University of Georgia Press · Athens

Publication of this book was made possible
by a generous anonymous gift.

Published by the University of Georgia Press
Athens, Georgia 30602
www.ugapress.org
© 2022 by Mary Carpenter
All rights reserved
Designed by Erin Kirk
Set in Miller Text with Caravan ornaments
Printed and bound by Versa Press
The paper in this book meets the guidelines for
permanence and durability of the Committee on
Production Guidelines for Book Longevity of the
Council on Library Resources.

Most University of Georgia Press titles are
available from popular e-book vendors.

Printed in the United States of America
26 25 24 23 22 C 5 4 3 2 1

Library of Congress Control Number: 2022930477
ISBN: 9780820360508 (hardback)
ISBN: 9780820360492 (ebook)

To my sons, Edmund and Oliver

Contents

Prologue

Lunch at St. Vincent's Grammar School for Girls in Savannah, Georgia, meant sharing. The giggling fifth-grade girls couldn't wait to see what their mothers had packed and then to pass around the sandwiches so anyone could take a nibble.

Before she left home one morning, Mary Flannery O'Connor carefully opened her sandwich and added several drops of cod liver oil, a thick brown liquid that many children were forced to swallow, a spoonful each day, in the 1920s and for decades to come. Cod liver oil was thought to bolster the body's ability to fight viruses and other diseases. The stuff tasted disgusting, but Mary Flannery knew it was harmless. She made sure not to add so much that the other girls could detect the strong fishy odor.

Mary Flannery wanted to teach her classmates a lesson. She didn't like to share, especially not her lunch. The cod liver oil would remind those girls who sampled Mary Flannery's sandwich that she was someone who did what she wanted, no matter what almost anyone thought. That day she succeeded: now her classmates certainly knew to watch out for Mary Flannery. She was more unusual than they'd suspected. Never again should they push her to join the sandwich exchange.

Knowing her own mind and sticking to her guns gave Mary Flannery a voice that was strong and distinctive when she began writing fiction. Writing under the name Flannery O'Connor, she worked hard every day. She wrote and re-wrote her stories for years if necessary, to get them exactly the way she wanted them to be told, or, as she put it, until she enjoyed reading them and no longer got bored.

At crucial points in her career, she risked angering two very influential people: the publisher who had already paid money in advance for her first novel and a prominent literary critic in the middle of a live TV interview. She refused to do what these men asked because she was so sure of what she wanted to say and how she wanted to say it.

Who doesn't wish to stand up to classmates, teachers, friends, family members, coworkers, and bosses, and tell them, "No, I don't want to do that" or "No, I don't agree"? Flannery O'Connor learned early on to take the best advantage of her quirky reputation, as she would eventually make the best of obstacles posed by her poor health, to become one of the most popular and successful fiction writers of the twentieth century.

Part I

Early Years, 1925–1937

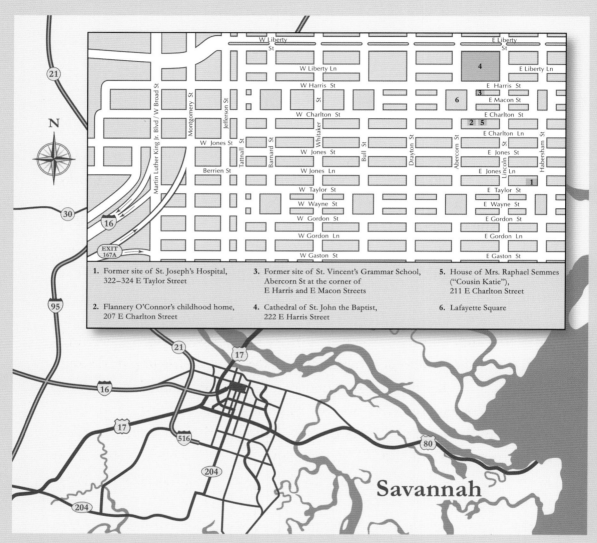

Figure 1.1 The O'Connor family lived on one of Savannah's twenty-four small squares (upper right, 2), across from the cathedral and a few steps away from Mary Flannery's school. Most of the O'Connors' neighbors were Catholic families.

Chapter One
Staring and Listening

Young Mary Flannery stood for hours at her parents' bedroom window. She had on the clunky supportive shoes, which she hated, so her mother wouldn't pester her to wear them. And she wore her "leave-me-alone" look, as she called it, to keep anyone from bothering her. She wanted to stand there, to look and to listen. She had no idea that spending hours paying close attention to her world was the best preparation possible for becoming a writer.

From her second-floor view over Lafayette Square, Mary Flannery liked to watch families stroll in the dusty light of warm spring evenings. Sometimes a car or horse-drawn carriage drove along the unpaved streets below, passing her narrow row house and the larger mansions that surrounded the square. Thin breezes came through now and then, heavy with humidity from the rivers that wound through the city of Savannah. Bells from the Cathedral of St. John the Baptist, which towered above Mary Flannery's house from across the square, rang out rich and heavy to mark the time.

The tight-knit cluster of Catholic families living around Lafayette Square knew each other well. Mary Flannery knew the men standing around the square shouting angrily, red-faced from the heat and from drinking. She recognized loud words like *president* and *unemployment*. She watched the young mothers below her window laughing together when they weren't feeding or quieting a crying baby.

Mary Flannery knew the rowdy boys thudding around the square's dirt lot with their noisy football games. She knew enough to steer clear

Figure 1.2 Mary Flannery read childhood books with a critical eye: she praised *Little Men* but considered *Alice's Adventures in Wonderland* "awful."

of them. She knew the girls from St. Vincent's School, also located on the square, who were whispering secrets she didn't much care about, although she liked it when one of her friends told her about them later.

Born on March 25, 1925, in the coastal city of Savannah, Mary Flannery O'Connor was called Mary or, more often, Mary Flannery in the southern manner of calling people by their first two names. What most of Mary Flannery's family wanted, along with everyone else who knew her, was for her to become a southern belle with ladylike clothes and agreeable manners, someone who didn't speak out or speak up for herself. But Mary Flannery had her own ideas. Later she wrote about how her mother "forced [me] to take dancing to throw me into the company of other children and to make me graceful. Nothing I hated worse than the company of other children and I vowed I'd see them all in hell before I would make the first graceful move."

Besides the heavy shoes, Mary Flannery wore braces on her teeth, which was unusual at the time because they were so expensive. But since her uncle was a dentist, he charged her parents less than the normal fee. In school and family photos, Mary Flannery stood out as the girl with the mischievous look, often wearing pants, while the others smiled in their skirts and dresses.

Another way Mary Flannery seemed odd to the residents of Lafayette Square was being an only child, because most Catholic families had many children. She later described herself as a "pigeon-toed, only-child with a receding chin and a you-leave-me-alone-or-I'll-bite-you complex." As

Figure 1.3 Mary Flannery's bedroom was downstairs from the claw-footed bathtub where she persuaded friends to sit and read aloud from stories she had written.

Figure 1.4 From a second-floor window of the O'Connor family's house,
Mary Flannery looked and listened to neighbors gathering in Lafayette Square below.

The Misfit

When people read the short story that has become Flannery O'Connor's most famous, "A Good Man Is Hard to Find," with its character called The Misfit, they wonder how much the young Mary Flannery had thought of herself as a child who did not fit in. In the story, a family on vacation in their car gets lost on a wooded dirt road. They encounter a band of three escaped criminals led by The Misfit.

The Misfit identifies himself as an outsider when he tells the grandmother,

> My daddy said I was a different breed of dog from my brothers and sisters. "You know," Daddy said, "it's some that can live their whole life out without asking about it and it's others has to know why it is, and this boy is one of the latters."

Mary Flannery was "one of the latters," someone who asks questions. Being different from other children made her familiar with the outsider's point of view. Later these differences helped her create unusual characters and write about what happens to people who are excluded and also to those who do the excluding. The misfit is a familiar character that appears often throughout Flannery O'Connor's short stories and novels.

"A Good Man Is Hard to Find," in O'Connor, *The Complete Stories*, 128–29.

such, she was free to spend a great deal of time by herself, observing and reflecting on everything around her.

At age six, Mary Flannery announced to her parents that she was no longer a child. As a result, she planned to call them by their first names, Regina and Ed. If Mary Flannery became impatient with her mother's socializing after church, she called in a loud, annoyed voice something like, "Come on, Regina, I'm ready to go home." People around Lafayette Square were shocked to hear a young girl speak to her mother that way.

While these scenes probably confirmed their opinion of Mary Flannery as a puzzling, unruly child, they also viewed Regina as an excessively indulgent mother.

Toward her daughter, Regina was both indulgent and overprotective. Regina Cline had grown up in a typically large Catholic family, one of sixteen children, because her father already had eight children from a previous marriage when he married her mother. Regina's family lived in the small Georgia town of Milledgeville, about a hundred miles west of Savannah, where Mary Flannery would attend high school and college. Regina took her daughter there for frequent visits, and they also spent time on the Cline family's farm just outside town. Why Regina had only one child and why she was so unusually protective of Flannery is not known, though some wondered whether she had a premonition about the illness that would seriously affect her family.

In Savannah, Regina insisted on walking her daughter the few dozen steps between her school and their house and church, all located around the same small square. Sometimes Regina even came to St. Vincent's to escort her daughter home for lunch. In contrast, Mary Flannery's friends and classmates walked around the neighborhood on their own and usually ate lunch at school.

Being considered different in the South meant being disapproved of. While Mary Flannery didn't care about that, what she did mind was the public spectacle Regina made by appearing at school so often and by telling the nuns what she didn't like about the school and their teaching. On the other hand, one of the nuns said later that Regina was supportive of her and the school.

Regina attracted more attention when she didn't permit Mary Flannery to visit other girls' homes. And Regina selected which girls could come over to play with her daughter; worse, she invited them herself. One day when a girl who had been invited brought an unapproved friend, Regina asked that girl to leave, which upset their well-mannered community.

Mary Flannery bristled at Regina's iron hand, although other girls' mothers were controlling too. They pushed their daughters to visit Mary

Flannery when they didn't want to. For these girls, summer trips to the farm belonging to Mary Flannery's cousins near Milledgeville were the most unpleasant. One day on the farm, Mary Flannery tied her guest to a chair, though she soon ran back to release her. And she tricked girls to walk into the muddy pigpen, though they usually caught on before things went too far. After visiting the farm, some girls begged their mothers not to make them return.

Occasionally, Mary Flannery fought back against Regina. On Savannah's stiflingly hot nights, she liked to push her twin bed over to the window in hope of catching a light breeze. Regina worried that the flat roof outside that window was too tempting and forbade her to move the bed. Every night Mary Flannery went ahead and moved it, and every morning Regina returned it to the center of the room.

Other times, Mary Flannery was unable to resist Regina, who wanted to educate her daughter about the world. Regina liked to take Mary Flannery to visit St. Mary's Home, an orphanage for girls, and also to invite the girls to the family's Lafayette Square house. Those experiences were "my first view of hell," Flannery wrote later. "Children know by instinct that hell is an absence of love."

At the same time, Mary Flannery had more freedom than many girls. Regina, though protective, was busy with chores at home and visits to friends and extended family. And Ed traveled frequently for his sales jobs.

Edward O'Connor grew up in Savannah. After college he enlisted in the Georgia National Guard and then fought in France during World War I. When the war was over, Ed worked as a distributor for his father's candy and tobacco business and invested in real estate. He met Regina Cline at a family wedding in 1922, and they married within months.

In 1929, the U.S. economy crashed, setting off the economic crisis known as the Great Depression, which would last more than ten years. Investors around the country had been paying ever-higher prices and taking out ever-bigger loans until, almost overnight, people lost confidence in the economy. They withdrew their money from banks and unloaded

King Cotton

In the early days of the United States, cotton was the main crop of the southern states, and southern port cities such as Savannah expanded with income from the cotton trade. Cotton required large numbers of laborers to do back-breaking work. To make a profit, southern farms relied on unpaid, enslaved workers.

When slavery became illegal following the Civil War and the Emancipation Proclamation, southern farmers struggled to bring in their crops. Freed black men and women who were unable to find jobs often had to return to the plantations for work. Some became sharecroppers, who farmed small plots of land and used a hefty portion of their crops to pay rent. Many others were arrested under new "vagrancy" laws that made it illegal to be jobless or homeless. Unable to pay court fees and fines, tens of thousands of black men and sometimes women were forced into "penal servitude," laboring without pay in industries like mining and on state roads and cotton plantations and elsewhere.

Soon afterward, a little beetle called the boll weevil began to harm cotton crops, rapaciously consuming cotton buds (or "bolls") and cotton flowers. By the early 1900s, the bugs had multiplied across the South, seriously damaging crops, and Savannah's port began its steep decline.

their investments, causing businesses around the country to fail and the stock market to crash. Throughout the 1930s, the economy continued to worsen until more than one fourth of the nation's workforce was unemployed. By 1932, farmers' incomes amounted to one third of what they had been, and many lost their farms.

The fortunes of the city of Savannah had started falling years earlier with the decline of the cotton trade. When Ed's income from sales and investments dwindled during the Depression, he traveled more often for work. At least the O'Connors had meat on the table. Help arrived from Regina's relative, whom Mary Flannery called Cousin Katie, who became a fairy godmother to her and her family.

Cousin Katie Semmes had inherited from her father the incredible sum of one million dollars (worth about ten million in early twenty-first-century terms). She lent the O'Connor family money to pay for their house at 207 East Charlton Street. The four-story row houses on Lafayette Square were so narrow that each floor included only two or three small rooms. Katie was wealthy enough to buy two houses just like the O'Connors' next door, one to live in and one to use as a garage for her electric car.

Cousin Katie would be one of many strong females who dominated Mary Flannery's childhood and may have helped motivate her to become a strong woman as well. Katie bestowed on Mary Flannery, at age five, a special gift of chickens, which brought her a surprising success, gave her a lifelong passion, and added to her image as an odd girl.

Chapter Two
Chickens

While many children had cats and dogs, Mary Flannery found them frightening. Instead, she played with the horses and pigs on the Clines' farm in central Georgia. Most of all, she adored chickens, which her family kept for eggs and sometimes meat in their tiny dirt backyard in Savannah. During Mary Flannery's childhood, people who bred chickens wanted to improve the birds' looks rather than the number of eggs they laid, in what was called "the chicken craze."

"When I was five . . . I began to collect chickens," Flannery wrote later. "I favored those with one green eye and one orange or with overlong necks and crooked combs." She brought her chickens indoors to put them down for naps in her old baby crib, called a Kiddie Koop. Made of wire mesh over a frame, the crib looked cold and unwelcoming for a human baby and much better suited to napping chickens. Later, Mary Flannery sewed a white coat with a lace collar and two buttons in back for the rooster she named Colonel Eggbert.

When Mary Flannery was still too young to start school, Cousin Katie bought her niece some fancy bantams. Bantams are small chickens that require less food and are thus cheaper to raise than the standard size bird. The bantams from Katie included a breed called Cochin, with fluffy plumage and fully feathered legs that exaggerated the chickens' size.

Mary Flannery figured out a lot about the intelligence of chickens, which scientists who studied learning and the brain didn't document until decades later, when they taught chicks to play peek-a-boo. Mary Flannery taught one of her own frizzle-feathered Cochin chickens to walk backward.

Figure 2.1 Mary Flannery kept Cochin chickens, a special breed known for their feathered legs and friendly nature, and she taught one to walk backward.

Figure 2.2 The Kiddie Koop, with its wire sides and top, was a child's crib that Mary Flannery used for her napping chickens.

When Cousin Katie heard about the backward-walking chicken, she became an early supporter of her niece's odd interests. Katie contacted Pathé News, producers of short newsreel films that were shown in schools and in movie theaters before the main feature. Pathé agreed to send a cameraman to Savannah. When he arrived at the O'Connor house, Mary Flannery had to prod and scold the chicken, which kicked up a lot of backyard dust and finally appeared to move backward. The film, called *Unique Chicken Goes in Reverse,* lasted less than two minutes but brought Mary Flannery national fame, or so she believed.

These chickens were important to Mary Flannery's future. She practiced walking like them, forward but also backward as in the Pathé newsreel. Regina said her daughter was a great mimic. Mary Flannery wrote so many stories about her treasured pets that one of the nuns at St. Vincent's School told her something like, "No more compositions about chickens."

But mostly she drew these chickens, "beginning at the tail, the same chicken over and over," she wrote. With each drawing of one gorgeous Cochin, Mary Flannery noticed a new wrinkle or feather design. She kept drawing until she believed she had discovered everything about that chicken. Sometimes she put drawings of her chickens under her father's breakfast napkin, and he carried them in his wallet to show friends.

One drawing that Mary Flannery created for Thanksgiving when she was six showed a happy turkey that appears completely unaware of the even happier man jumping alongside who intends to eat him. The drawing is an early example of Mary Flannery's cartoons, which by high school would begin to make her better known and appreciated.

In her own way, Mary Flannery was preparing to become a writer. Later she advised young writers to do "anything that helps you see, anything that makes you look. There is nothing that doesn't require [the writer's] attention." And, she told them, "The writer should never be ashamed of staring."

At the same time, Mary Flannery read lots of books. When she was very young, Ed and Regina respected their daughter's taste enough to allow her to write her opinions, often harsh ones, inside the covers of the few books she owned.

Figure 2.3 Mary Flannery's Thanksgiving cartoon portrays a happy turkey unaware of the even happier man who intends to eat him.

Fantasies like *Alice in Wonderland* terrified Mary Flannery, perhaps a sign of her vivid imagination. She also avoided walking through nearby Colonial Cemetery, which most neighborhood kids used as a shortcut to Saturday afternoon movies, and instead took the long way around.

While most girls she knew spent their summers outdoors in Savannah or in the nearby countryside, Mary Flannery preferred to stay inside and read. Lucky enough to have relatives in Georgia's capital of Atlanta, she enrolled in a vacation book club one summer at a public library in the city and remained there with her cousins while she completed the reading list.

The books Mary Flannery admired most in her childhood were *The Collected Works of Edgar Allan Poe*, which her family owned, especially volume eight, called *The Humorous Tales*. The O'Connors also possessed an old encyclopedia in which Mary Flannery read about classical mythology. "The only good things I read when I was a child were the Greek and Roman myths," she wrote later. "The rest of what I read was Slop with a capital S . . . followed by the Edgar Allan Poe period which lasted for years."

⬤ Childhood Books

Books Mary Flannery read as a young child—inscribed with her often-harsh handwritten comments—are on display for visitors to read throughout her family's Savannah house, and include comments such as the following:

The Five Little Peppers and How They Grew, by Margaret Sidney
Mary Flannery wrote: "this is a first rate book an it blongs to M.F. O'Connor an don't fiddle with it."

Little Men, by Louisa May Alcott
Mary Flannery wrote: "First rate, splendid."

Fairy Babies, (author unknown)
Mary Flannery wrote: "not a very good book."

Alice's Adventures in Wonderland, by Lewis Carroll
Mary Flannery wrote: "Awful. I couldn't read this book."

In Poe's stories, the humor is silly slapstick filled with puns, including characters like Miss Fibalittle and tales like "The Duc de l'Omelette" (The Duke of the Omelet). But much of Poe's writing has a dark edge, with characters who are conceited or bullies and are eventually punished by eternal misery or death. One of Mary Flannery's favorite Poe stories, "The Man That Was Used Up," makes fun of a man who is vain about his exceptionally handsome looks. When a visitor shows up early one morning, he finds, instead of the handsome man, an "exceedingly odd-looking bundle of something." It turns out the man cared so much about his appearance that he had destroyed his own limbs, his hair, and even his voice and replaced them with fakes.

Despite all her reading, Mary Flannery misbehaved too often to be considered a good student. Once she brought a tomato as a gift for the nuns, making fun of the traditional teacher's-pet gift of a shiny red apple.

When she shot rubber bands from her braces across the classroom, the nuns struck her hands with a wooden ruler as punishment. What enraged the nuns most, though, was when she acted "forward" by talking to them as her equals. From an early age, Mary Flannery believed she understood as much as almost any adult, about the world and about God. Ed and Regina did nothing to quash their daughter's confidence.

When she was in fifth grade, Mary Flannery one day made up her mind that she would no longer bother about correct spelling. She had always gotten near-perfect report cards, but now her grades plummeted. At the next report, she explained to Regina about her geography grade of 85, "Sister said that would have been a 95 except for my spelling and in history I got a 64. In spelling of course I got a 40."

For the rest of her life, Mary Flannery remained what she called a "very innocent speller," ignoring criticism from teachers, editors, and her mother. But sometimes her misspellings seemed like sly jokes made on purpose. After she became a famous writer, Flannery O'Connor still wrote "bisnis" or "bidnis" (business) especially when people took their "bidnis" a little too seriously.

Looking back on her childhood, she wrote that she was no "angle" (angel), this time making fun of herself. And she wrote about "the startling effect" of a woman who "dyed her hair the color of funnytoor [furniture] polish."

Beginning in third grade, Mary Flannery and her friends formed the Merriweather Girls, a group that gathered at the playhouse in the O'Connors' backyard and ran around with the family's chickens and ducks. Some girls came on Saturday mornings to eat Regina's fresh-baked gingerbread men and listen to their favorite radio show, *Let's Pretend*, which each week broadcast one story or fairy tale using child actors for the voices.

Sometimes Mary Flannery led a visiting friend upstairs to the third-floor bathroom. There she had prepared the empty claw-footed bathtub with two oversized pillows decorated with brightly colored stitches. She convinced her guest to sit in the tub with her and listen while she read aloud from her favorite fairy tales, collected by the Brothers Grimm. The

Mary Flannery's Journal

Many writers keep a journal to record observations and reflections, which they might use for future projects. The summer Mary Flannery was twelve, she wrote in a tiny notebook, about three inches by four, to record gripes using her special spelling. She began her journal with a warning to snoopers: "I know some folks that don't mind thier own bisnis." In one entry, she shrugged off her failures at school, writing: "Teacher said I dident know how to spell what of it?"

In another, she wrote: "I do not see much use of A's B's & D's in Ari [arithmetic]: I can add and sub. [subtract] and mul. [multiply]. . . what good'll it do me?

O'Connor, *Habit of Being*, xi–xiv, 96n.

versions in her book of *Grimms' Fairy Tales*, unlike those revised in later years, ended badly. The princess in "The Frog Prince" slammed the frog against a wall instead of kissing him, and the "Pied Piper of Hamelin" led most of the town's children into a mountain, never to be heard from again.

For another bathtub activity, Mary Flannery read aloud from stories she had written, many concerning her chickens, or she requested that her friends do the reading. Every few sentences, she asked the reader to stop and "read that over again." To her ear, some lines needed a little more work. Mary Flannery realized that the girls didn't always enjoy sitting in the bathtub, but her friends were good actors. Hearing her own words read aloud in their soft, syrupy Savannah accents helped Mary Flannery immensely as she worked to improve her writing.

Unusual for parents of that time, Ed was such a strong supporter of his daughter and her writing that he paid to print seven copies of a little book she had written. *My Relitives* (relatives) was a collection of satirical stories about Mary Flannery's aunts, uncles, and cousins. Ed O'Connor was the first person who might have predicted his daughter would one day become a published author. When that came to pass, she named her father as her inspiration.

Flannery admitted later that *My Relitives* contained portraits that were "uncomfortably close" to actual family members and that the book was not well received. Regina disapproved, saying later about the little book, "No one was spared." If her daughter was going to write, Regina thought the subject should be something pious or spiritual, and Catholic doctrine would be best.

Flannery O'Connor's later fiction did address Catholic doctrine but in a way that many Catholics, including Regina, could not or would not recognize. First, though, Mary Flannery struggled to endure some of the less pleasant aspects of her very strict Catholic and very southern childhood.

Chapter Three
Catholic and Southern

When Mary Flannery was a young girl, being Catholic almost anywhere in the South meant being treated like an outsider and second-class citizen. The religious beliefs of Catholics were unfamiliar to most southerners, who belonged to Protestant faiths like Baptist or Methodist. In the 1920s and 1930s, employment notices posted around Savannah said, "Catholics need not apply." Catholic families kept to their own neighborhoods, and many clustered around Lafayette Square.

The Catholic religion enveloped Mary Flannery every day of her childhood and gave her beliefs that would guide her writing and her life. The tall steeples of the Cathedral of St. John the Baptist across the square from her house loomed overhead whenever she looked out her window or walked out her front door, and its bells tolled morning, noon, and night.

Under the cathedral's soaring arches, Mary Flannery attended Mass every Sunday and many other days as well. Sunlight colored with the blues and reds of the tall stained-glass windows bathed Mary Flannery in her pew. She heard the majestic organ chords and sang the traditional hymns. She repeated the daily prayers and breathed the fragrant smoky incense. She stared at the Stations of the Cross, fourteen sculptures that showed Jesus carrying the heavy cross on his long walk toward crucifixion and death, displayed along the cathedral's walls.

Prayers punctuated her long Catholic school days as well as Sundays. The faces of Jesus and the Virgin Mary hung on Mary Flannery's bedroom walls, somber religious prints that she saw every day of her childhood. Stories about Jesus and Mary told and retold in church and in her

Figure 3.1 The Cathedral of St. John the Baptist loomed above Mary Flannery's house from across the square, with the tallest twin steeples in Savannah and bells that rang morning, noon, and night.

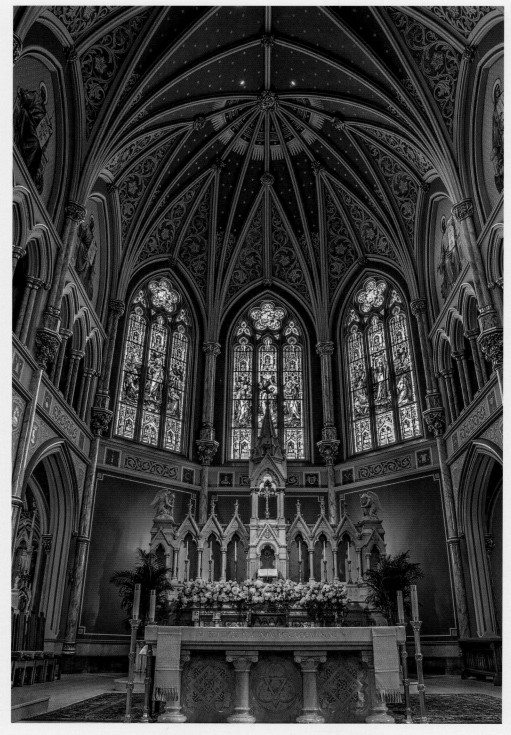

Figure 3.2 At the Cathedral of St. John the Baptist, Mary Flannery attended Mass in the imposing interior lit by colorful stained-glass windows with fourteen sculptures of the Stations of the Cross along one wall.

religious classes at St. Vincent's School exposed Mary Flannery every day to the religious traditions of storytelling.

The fourth floor of the O'Connor house was empty except when the family rented to boarders. Between the ages of eight and twelve, Mary Flannery went up there to fight with her guardian angel, in the Catholic religion a heavenly spirit assigned by God to keep each person from harm and guide them to good thoughts and actions. "It was my habit to seclude myself in a locked room every so often and with a fierce (and evil) face, whirl around in a circle with my fist knotted, socking the angel. . . . I'm sure I even kicked at him," Flannery wrote later. Though she never revealed the reasons for these fights or their outcomes, she later admitted that "you couldn't hurt an angel, but I would have been happy to know I had dirtied his feathers."

For Mary Flannery, angels and God were as real as she was. While many people believe that the wafer and sip of wine they receive at Holy Communion services are symbols of the body and blood of Christ, she did not agree. When someone later referred to the wafer as a symbol, Flannery O'Connor wrote a friend, "I then said, in a very shaky voice, 'Well if it's a symbol, to hell with it.'" Along with most strict Catholics, she believed these were the actual body and actual blood of Christ.

For Flannery O'Connor, the central mystery of life was that human beings exist on Earth and that their existence has "been found by God to be worth dying for." She made her stories violent and scary, she said, to shock both characters and readers into feeling God's presence everywhere in the world, to show them this mystery. "Violence is strangely capable of returning my characters to reality and preparing them to accept their moment of Grace," she wrote.

At the end of fifth grade, Mary Flannery left St. Vincent's, because her mother transferred her to Sacred Heart School for Girls. No one knows for sure how Mary Flannery reacted to the new school, but she might not have been enthusiastic about one of Regina's reasons for the move, what her mother regarded as a higher class of students at Sacred Heart. Most Sacred Heart families were "lace curtain," wealthier Irish, which was how the O'Connor and Cline families saw themselves. In contrast,

Violence in Flannery O'Connor's Writing

Violent confrontations often provoke Flannery's characters to develop more positive and generous feelings toward all kinds of people, from criminals and foreigners to those who are pretentious, vain, or hypocritical.

In "A Good Man Is Hard to Find," the criminal gang led by The Misfit takes children into the woods. Soon afterward, the sound of gunshots suggests that the children have been killed. When their selfish grandmother hears the shots, she tries to save her own life by being kind to The Misfit, saying to him, "Why you're one of my babies . . . one of my own children." When she reaches out to touch him, for that one moment, she becomes a caring and compassionate person.

In "Revelation," a mother in a doctor's waiting room complains that her college-age daughter, sitting nearby, is "ungrateful . . . just criticizes and complains all day long." When an insensitive and racist pig farmer named Mrs. Turpin agrees, the daughter hurls a book that hits Mrs. Turpin over her eye, lunges and sinks her fingers into Mrs. Turpin's neck, and calls her "an old wart hog." That violence seems to alter Mrs. Turpin's racist views, because later that day, she has a vision of crowds, Black people mixed together with those who are white, who seem to be "rumbling toward heaven."

O'Connor, "A Good Man," in *Complete Stories*, 132; "Revelation," *Complete Stories*, 409, 508.

many Lafayette Square Irish families, dubbed "shanty" after the roughly built shacks of the Irish working class, were more recent, poorer immigrants. When Regina drove Mary Flannery the twenty blocks to Sacred Heart in Cousin Katie's electric car, her schoolmates rushed out to watch the unfamiliar, expensive vehicle glide silently by.

Changing Mary Flannery's school was part of Regina's ongoing effort to make her daughter a southern belle. This stereotyped southern female was valued less for her talents or achievements than for her smoothly curled hair, her slim waist, and her desire to please others. Besides selecting friends for her daughter Regina arranged for her to have lessons in dancing and piano. In Mary Flannery's memory, Regina spanked her only once, and that was to force her to wear stockings for her first piano recital.

But the day Regina made her wear a flowered dress and attend a dance, Mary Flannery fought back. She filled her mouth with snuff, a finely ground tobacco that men sometimes stuffed inside their lower lips but more often inhaled. Snuff was not something most women took, especially not a southern lady. Regina's outrage can only be imagined.

Across the square from the O'Connors, a sprawling mansion built before the Civil War had been the home of Juliette Gordon Low, founder of the Girl Scouts of America, in which Mary Flannery participated reluctantly. The highlight for her occurred the day a flock of birds swooped, landed, and got in line behind the marching girls. The scouts slowly realized that Mary Flannery's pet ducks had located the troop and joined them.

Although the Civil War ended in 1865, sixty years before Mary Flannery's birth, her relatives and neighbors continued to talk about the war. They spoke in romantic terms about the "southern way of life," which the Confederate army had fought to preserve, without acknowledging how that way of life depended on the cruel and inhumane treatment of millions of enslaved people. Mary Flannery did not like or agree with this romantic view, as she wrote later: "I sure am sick of the Civil War."

Before the war came to plantations near Savannah, enslaved workers were forced to harvest cotton and rice in vast, swelteringly hot fields, working from before sunrise until after dark. Often-brutal overseers beat or whipped those who disobeyed or were caught praying or learning to read and write. Enslaved people were bought and sold at auctions that separated small children from their parents and moved loved ones far apart, usually never to see each other again.

Legal slavery ended when the Thirteenth Amendment to the U.S. Constitution took effect in December 1865, but Mary Flannery grew up in a very racist Deep South. New, unjust laws forbade "vagrancy," defined as being without a job or fixed address. The laws led to the arrest of tens

Figure 3.3 Many antebellum (meaning "before the war") mansions had grand facades with columns and wide verandas for southern rituals like afternoon tea and mint julep cocktails. The Civil War and the poverty that followed destroyed most of these mansions throughout the southern states, except in Savannah, which preserved the look and feel of the Old South. The Andrew Low House, on Lafayette Square across from the O'Connors', welcomes visitors today.

of thousands of formerly enslaved people, both men and women, called freedmen. Unable to afford fines and court costs, freedmen worked in what was called "penal servitude" for the county or for private employers, without payment and often for the rest of their lives.

Along the country roads of Georgia, Mary Flannery saw the chain gangs of Black freedmen bound together while working, like enslaved people under an overseer, on roadside farms or in construction. In Savannah, African Americans walked the streets for hours carrying heavy baskets of vegetables, crabs, and oysters for sale. Many others worked long, grueling days as servants in private houses, and often slept on bare wooden floors.

Mary Flannery also lived during time of the "Jim Crow" laws that required Black people to use separate water fountains and sit in the back of public buses. And the 1920s of her childhood were peak years for the Ku Klux Klan, whose members asserted that the only true Americans were white, of English ancestry, and Protestant. On an aggressive mission to rid the country of African Americans, these terrorists were linked to thousands of lynchings—murders of Black people often by hanging them from trees.

The look and feel of the Old South may have persisted longer in Savannah than elsewhere, because the city was one of the few in the South left undamaged after the Civil War. The most often repeated Civil War tale concerned the day General William Tecumseh Sherman and his Union army arrived in town on their famous March to the Sea, burning everything for three hundred miles, including most of the city of Atlanta. But Savannah, with its pastel mansions nestled among flowering bushes and live oak trees and twenty-four squares that dated to colonial times, charmed the general. Sherman sent a telegram offering the city as a Christmas gift to President Lincoln, and Savannah was spared.

Mary Flannery disliked the sanitized and dishonest stories of the Old South told by sentimental books and movies of the time. The best-selling novel *Gone with the Wind*, by fellow Georgian Margaret Mitchell, came out when Mary Flannery was eleven. The novel brims with fond descriptions of grand cotton plantations and Confederate heroes but makes light of the

⬟ *Gone with the Wind*

Gone with the Wind, a 1936 novel by Margaret Mitchell, takes place during the Civil War and the period that followed, called Reconstruction. The novel depicts a wealthy cotton plantation and the family living there—before the Civil War; during the war, which destroys the plantation and tears apart the family; and during the postwar period both on the plantation and in Atlanta.

The book labels the murderous Ku Klux Klan a "tragic necessity," and the film shows enslaved servants like Prissy lavishing excessive praise on their white employers. Despite overly glamorizing a racist society, both the book and the film remained popular throughout Georgia into the twenty-first century.

In Flannery's story "A Late Encounter with the Enemy," a self-centered old man with no memory of his years fighting in the Civil War takes a false name and the false rank of general and wears an elaborate costume for a premiere of *Gone with the Wind*. Later he attends another ceremony using the same false name, rank, and costume of the general that represent racist "old traditions! Dignity! Honor!" like the film does. Left sitting in his wheelchair for too long in the hot sun, the man dies unnoticed.

O'Connor, "A Late Encounter with the Enemy," in *Complete Stories*, 405.

suffering of enslaved people. The movie based on the book opened three years later, set box office records that would stand for decades to come, and (although people argue about this) remains the highest-grossing film in history.

Although Mary Flannery refused to act the southern belle, in high school she became close to pretty, flirty Mary Virginia Harrison, the kind of friend Regina always wanted for her daughter. The two girls made an odd pair but shared the best kind of friendship. One was different enough from the other to make things interesting, and as friends they forgave

Race and Class in Flannery O'Connor's Stories

Flannery O'Connor's most unlikable characters judge other people and themselves based on class, usually determined by their money and possessions, and by their skin color. In letters to friends, Flannery sometimes used the racist vocabulary of her time and place. On the other hand, in the fiction she wrote, Flannery reflected deeply about the pain that racism causes, and about the ignorance and hypocrisy of white people about race.

In "Everything That Rises Must Converge," a short story about two women, one white and one Black, who are riding on a city bus with their sons, the white mother "would not ride the buses by herself at night since they had been integrated." When she says, "I most certainly do know who I am. . . . You remain what you are. Your great-grandfather had a plantation and two hundred slaves," the white mother shows that she views owning other people as a sign of status, not of shame.

In "Revelation," the pig farmer Ruby Turpin lies in bed at night "naming the classes of people." She places herself and her husband close to the top, above "most colored people . . . white-trash . . . [and] home-owners," because the Turpins are "home-*and*-land owners."

In "A Good Man Is Hard to Find," when the grandmother tries to convince the character called The Misfit not to shoot her, she tells him he has "good blood! I know you wouldn't shoot a lady. I know you come from nice people."

O'Connor, "Everything That Rises Must Converge," in *Complete Stories*, 405; "Revelation," in *Complete Stories*, 407–8; O'Connor, "A Good Man Is Hard to Find," in *Complete Stories*, 131–32.

these differences. When Mary Virginia invited Mary Flannery to dance parties at her house, sometimes she accepted.

Once, Mary Flannery agreed to go on a double date with Mary Virginia and her boyfriend; Mary Flannery's date would be the boyfriend's cousin. Mary Flannery spoke little the entire evening but then suddenly stamped her foot and said, "My dad-gum foot's gone to sleep!" Such country expressions, along with the misspellings, were part of Mary Flannery's rebellion against minding the rules and manners required of well-bred southern girls.

By the time she was a teenager, Mary Flannery felt suffocated by the Old South. She believed she needed to move to another part of the country, far away, if she was going to do anything with her life. Until she finished college, she had to stay in Georgia; after that, she would leap at the first opportunity to head north.

Part II
Education, 1937–1945

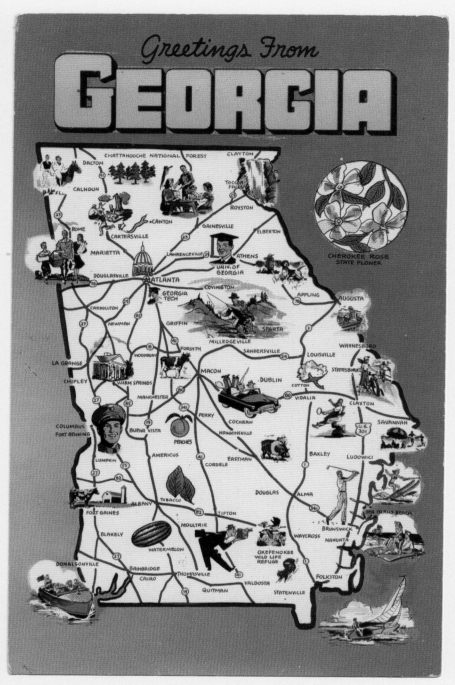

Figure 4.1 During Mary Flannery's childhood, the O'Connor family traveled back and forth between Savannah and the Cline house and farm in Milledgeville where Mary Flannery's mother grew up, then lived briefly in Atlanta, and finally moved permanently to Milledgeville when Mary Flannery was twelve.

Chapter Four
Cartooning

At age twelve, Mary Flannery worked with her mother to pack up the Savannah house. By 1937, eight years of the Great Depression had ruined Ed O'Connor's real estate business. Cousin Katie again helped the family with money until Ed found work in Atlanta, and then the O'Connors needed to move.

Leaving that house upset Mary Flannery more than leaving behind friends and everything else in Savannah, because she believed it contained her "entire childhood." Later she said, "When I was 12, I made up my mind absolutely that I would not get any older . . . I was a very ancient twelve."

For the last months of seventh grade, Mary Flannery attended a new school in Atlanta, where half the city's men were unemployed because of the Depression. Mary Flannery saw hungry men waiting in long food lines and children in tattered clothes begging in the streets. Men who had no work came to her family's back door asking to do small jobs in exchange for food.

For the next two years, while Ed stayed in Atlanta for his job, Mary Flannery traveled with her mother back and forth between the city and Regina's family home in Milledgeville. They made the hundred-mile trip past unpainted houses with junked cars in the yards. They saw families in battered pickup trucks with their entire household belongings tied onto the back beds, driving the roads in search of work.

At the beginning of Mary Flannery's tenth-grade year, the O'Connor family finally settled in Milledgeville, deep in the red clay country of middle Georgia, so remote it could be reached only "by bus or buzzard," she

Figure 4.2 Regina O'Connor made sure her daughter participated in social activities, but in most photos Mary Flannery (top row, middle) looks less than pleased to be there.

wrote later. Small-town Milledgeville may have accepted Mary Flannery's quirkiness better than the cities of Savannah and Atlanta, where people behaved more properly and judged each other more severely. Certainly, Milledgeville gave her many of the eccentric southern characters and thick, drawling Georgia accents that later fueled her writing.

In Milledgeville, the O'Connors moved into the house at 311 Green Street that belonged to Regina's family and was surrounded by a grassy, tree-shaded yard. The mansion, elegant enough to serve as a temporary governor's residence in the mid-1800s, was soon after the Civil War purchased by Mary Flannery's grandfather Peter Cline. Enslaved workers had carved by hand the massive white columns standing two stories tall along the house's facade.

Ed was spending more time with his family in Milledgeville but he began to tire easily and often had a midday nap, leading townspeople to suspect he might be lazy. He was soon diagnosed with a disease called lupus. Lupus causes the body's immune system, which is supposed to fend off infections like viruses, to attack the body's own organs, such as the heart and kidneys. But little was known about lupus at the time, and there was no treatment.

To create her own art studio, Mary Flannery took over the vast third floor of the Green Street house, with windows that gave her a 360-degree view over the town of Milledgeville. Two blocks to the south she saw the leafy trees of Memory Hill Cemetery shading graves of townspeople and Confederate soldiers. To the east flowed the wide, murky Oconee River, placid except after spring storms, when it became swollen and rushing. Down a long hilly road from town spread the massive buildings of the Georgia Lunatic, Idiot, and Epileptic Asylum, words used in those days to describe people with mental illnesses. At night, screams from the patients, mostly women, reached great distances through the quiet Georgia countryside.

With no Catholic school in town, Mary Flannery attended Peabody High School, located one block north of her new home. She didn't approve of Peabody's system of "progressive education," which allowed students to create their own academic programs. "One did not read if one did not wish to," she said, "I did not wish to." She expected school to do the teaching and thought Peabody failed to do so.

Nonetheless, at Peabody fifteen-year-old Mary Flannery began to be noticed for her talent and her humor. After Regina contacted the faculty adviser for the school newspaper, the *Peabody Palladium*, to talk about her daughter's art, the paper began printing Mary Flannery's cartoons.

The Thanksgiving cartoon Mary Flannery had drawn at age six showed early on that she had mastered the skills of storytelling, the same ones required for good cartooning. Catching the "rabbit," as she called it, involved getting to the heart of a complex idea by looking at one situation from several different points of view. And it required finding the humor. Mary Flannery liked to show the pleasure of one person or animal leading to the downfall of another, as well as the blindness of victims to their fate.

After catching the rabbit, Mary Flannery chose which elements to put in the image and whether to add words. While the Thanksgiving drawing

"These two express the universal feeling of heart-brokenness over school closing."

Figure 4.3 In Mary Flannery's cartoons, students appear eager to avoid school activities or to leave school altogether.

captured a complete joke without words, by high school Mary Flannery often added humorous captions. The cartooning skills that she developed, starting in childhood and through college, would help Flannery O'Connor find the unusual voice for her fiction that was clear, sometimes dark, and almost always funny.

Mary Flannery created cartoons with pen and ink, pencil, and charcoal, but her preferred medium was the linoleum cut, or block.

In her second year at Peabody, Mary Flannery was promoted to art editor of the *Palladium*. One friend described her as a wit with a little twinkle in her eye as if to say, "I know something you don't." Mary Flannery also wrote essays and stories for the newspaper. In her senior year, after she won a statewide essay contest sponsored by an Atlanta department store, she told the *Palladium* reporter that she'd begun writing at age six and that her ambition was "to keep right on writing, particularly satires."

Mary Flannery entertained the students in her Peabody home economics class, where girls learned homemaking skills such as cooking and sewing while the boys took woodworking or shop. With a "home ec" assignment to sew an entire outfit, Mary Flannery arrived in class with her duck

Linoleum Block Prints: Mary Flannery O'Connor's Cartoons

Linoleum block prints are created by artists using blocks of linoleum, a rubbery, flexible material made from ground cork, sawdust, and other substances, which was once commonly used on floors and kitchen counters.

When warmed on a hot plate, "linoleum cuts like butter . . . quick and easy," according to *Flannery O'Connor: The Cartoons*. The tricky part of making prints is to cut an image in the linoleum that must be the mirror or reverse of the final design.

After the image has been cut, the linoleum block is covered with ink and pressed onto paper, either by hand or using a block printing press. The final image appears as white areas and lines against a dark inked background.

Barry Moser, introduction to O'Connor, *Flannery O'Connor: The Cartoons*, viii.

Aloysius marching behind her in his new finery: gray shorts with a white shirt, a jacket, and a red bow tie. She made up funny stories about this duck, who accompanied her to Milledgeville Girl Scout meetings.

For her high school art class, Mary Flannery brought another duck, Herman, so she could paint his portrait. She also worked on a new little book called *Mistaken Identity*, about Herman and the efforts to find this duck a wife. As she wrote, "the point of the story came to me when Herman laid an egg"; afterward, the duck was renamed Henrietta.

The voices of strong women that filled the Green Street house sounded a lot like the female characters who later appeared in Flannery O'Connor's writing. Besides Mary Flannery and her mother, the house's residents included two of Regina's unmarried sisters, Mary and Katie Cline (not the Katie who bought the special chickens). Mary, who was tall, thin, and fierce looking, was called "Sister" or "Matriarch" and ran the

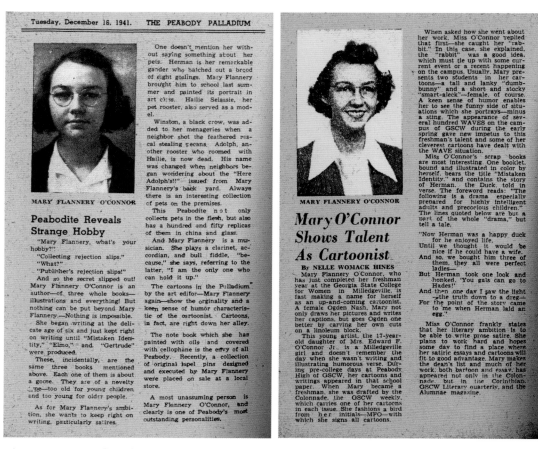

Tuesday, December 16, 1941.   THE PEABODY PALLADIUM

MARY FLANNERY O'CONNOR

Peabodite Reveals Strange Hobby

"Mary Flannery, what's your hobby?"

"Collecting rejection slips."

"What?"

"Publisher's rejection slips!"

And so the secret slipped out! Mary Flannery O'Connor is an author—of three whole books—illustrations and everything! But nothing can be put beyond Mary Flannery.—Nothing is impossible.

She began writing at the delicate age of six and just kept right on writing until "Mistaken Identity," "Elmo," and "Gertrude" were produced.

These, incidentally, are the same three books mentioned above. Each one of them is about a goose. They are of a novelty ,type—too old for young children and too young for older people.

As for Mary Flannery's ambition, she wants to keep right on writing, particularly satires.

One doesn't mention her without saying something about her pets. Herman is her remarkable gander who hatched out a brood of eight goslings. Mary Flannery brought him to school last summer and painted its portrait in art class. Hailie Selassie, her pet rooster, also served as a model.

Winston, a black crow, was added to her menageries when a neighbor shot the feathered rascal stealing pecans. Adolph, another rooster who roomed with Hailie, is now dead. His name was changed when neighbors began wondering about the "Here Adolph's!!" issued from Mary Flannery's back yard. Always there is an interesting collection of pets on the premises.

This Peabodite not only collects pets in the flesh, but also has a hundred and fifty replicas of them in china and glass.

And Mary Flannery is a musician. She plays a clarinet, accordian, and bull fiddle, "because," she says, referring to who can hold it up."

The cartoons in the Palladium by the art editor—Mary Flannery again—show the orginality and a keen sense of humor characteristic of the cartoonist. Cartoons, in fact, are right down her alley.

The note book which she has painted with oils and covered with cellophane is the envy of all Peabody. Recently, a collection of original lapel pins designed and executed by Mary Flannery were placed on sale at a local store.

A most unassuming person is Mary Flannery O'Connor, and clearly is one of Peabody's most outstanding personalities.

MARY FLANNERY O'CONNOR

Mary O'Connor Shows Talent As Cartoonist

By NELLE WOMACK HINES

Mary Flannery O'Connor, who has just completed her freshman year at the Georgia State College for Women in Milledgeville, is fast making a name for herself as an up-and-coming cartoonist. A female Ogden Nash, Mary not only draws her pictures and writes her captions, but goes Ogden one better by carving her own cuts on a linoleum block.

This young artist, the 17-year-old daughter of Mrs. Edward F. O'Connor Jr., is a Milledgeville girl and doesn't remember the day when she wasn't writing and illustrating humorous verse. During pre-college days at Peabody High of GSCW, her cartoons and writings appeared in that school paper. When Mary became a freshman, she was drafted by the Colonnade, the GSCW weekly, which carries one of her cartoons in each issue. She fashions a bird from her initials—MFO—with which she signs all cartoons.

When asked how she went about her work, Miss O'Connor replied that first she caught her "rabbit." In this case, she explained, the "rabbit" was a good idea, which must tie up with some current event or a recent happening on the campus. Usually, Mary presents two students in her cartoons—a tall and lanky "dumbbunny"—female, of course. A keen sense of humor enables her to see the funny side of situations which she portrays—minus a sting. The appearance of several hundred WAVES on the campus of GSCW during the early spring gave new impetus to this freshman's talent and some of her cleverest cartoons have dealt with the WAVE situation.

Miss O'Connor's scrap books are most interesting. One booklet, bound and illustrated in color by herself, bears the title "Mistaken Identity," and contains the story of Herman, the Duck, told in verse. The foreword reads: "The following is a drama especially prepared for highly intelligent adults and precocious children." The lines quoted below are but a part of the whole "drama," but tell a tale.

"Now Herman was a happy duck
for he enjoyed life.
Until we thought it would be
nice if he could have a wife.
And so, we bought him three of
them, they all were perfect ladies—
But Herman took one look and
honked, 'You gals can go to Hades!'
And then one day I saw the light
—the truth down to a dreg—
For the point of the story came
to me when Herman laid an egg."

Miss O'Connor frankly states that her literary ambition is to be able to write prose satire. She plans to work hard and hopes some day to find a place where her satiric essays and cartoons will fit to good advantage. Mary makes the dean's list and much of her work, both cartoon and essay, has appeared not only in the Colonnade, but in the Corinthian, GSCW Literary quarterly, and the Alumnae magazine.

Figures 4.4a and 4.4b For her talents at drawing and writing, Mary Flannery made the news in both her high school paper, the *Palladium,* and in a local city newspaper, the *Macon News and Telegraph.*

household. Katie worked at the post office, and Mary Flannery dubbed her "The Duchess" for her regal appearance in her fur-collared coat. Mary Flannery's great-aunt Gertie also lived there briefly.

Some weekends, her Uncle Bernard drove out from Atlanta where he worked as a doctor, and Ed O'Connor began to spend more time in Milledgeville between jobs. Soon Ed stopped working altogether and was sometimes too exhausted to get out of bed. His untreated lupus was "a death sentence," Flannery said later, though she didn't understand that at the time. Still, she worried constantly about her father.

On the afternoon of February 1, 1941, Mary Flannery would have returned from school to find the house unnaturally quiet. She probably had saved a funny story to tell Ed about her school-with-no-school-work. Entering her father's bedroom, Mary Flannery would have seen her mother and aunts sitting in a silence that was unusual for them. One look at Ed's face would tell her that he had died. Her father was only forty-five years old.

Later she said that the death of her "best friend" had been like a bullet in the side. Ed O'Connor was buried in Memory Hill Cemetery not long before Mary Flannery's sixteenth birthday. Working in her third-floor studio during the months and years afterward, she could look out over the cemetery and think about her father.

The following fall, the mailman delivered three books that Mary Flannery had paid to be printed: *Elmo* and *Gertrude*, tales of her geese, and *Mistaken Identity* about Herman/Henrietta. The publication of *Mistaken Identity*, filled with drawings of the duck, at first posing more like a male but at the end nesting on her eggs, led to an article in a nearby city newspaper headlined "Mary O'Connor Shows Talent as Cartoonist."

Mary Flannery said these books were "too old for young children and too young for older people." Regina still complained that her daughter's writing was not serious or religious. In many of Flannery O'Connor's later stories, the mother character is bossy and critical, and often the husband or father is missing.

With printing of these three new books, Mary Flannery missed her father more than ever. She thought Ed would have been proud to see her carry on what he'd started ten years earlier when he arranged for the small private printing of *My Relitives*.

"My father wanted to write but had not the time or money or training or any of the opportunities I have had," she later wrote. "Whatever I do in the way of writing makes me extra happy in the thought that it is a fulfillment of what he wanted to do himself." While cartooning continued to hone her sharp wit, Mary Flannery was also beginning the hard work of a serious education.

Chapter Five
At College

When Mary Flannery graduated from Peabody High School in the spring of 1942, she did not leave town for college. Instead, she walked across a wide green lawn from her school to attend the Georgia State College for Women. At that time, Georgia College was accepting students for a special program that compressed the traditional four college years into three. The United States had entered World War II after the Japanese bombed the naval base at Pearl Harbor the previous December, and needed women to finish college as soon as possible to fill the jobs of men who'd left to fight.

Almost every girl from Mary Flannery's high school class remained in Milledgeville to attend Georgia College, where many of their mothers had gone before them. During the war, families were reluctant to have their daughters travel far away or to pay the higher tuitions elsewhere. Mary Flannery continued to live at home with Regina and the Cline aunts.

Among highlights at Cline family lunches were silver platters of steaming corn, sweet potatoes, fried chicken, and biscuits. Arrangements of brightly colored roses and honeysuckle brought sweet fragrances into the dining room.

Although Regina expected her daughter to attend family gatherings, Mary Flannery often wished she could keep working on her cartoons, and she later said, "These things are fine for the people that like them and the people that don't, as my mother tells me, are just peculiar."

"These things" improved for Mary Flannery when her four Boston girl cousins visited, and the group laughed and talked for hours together in rocking chairs on the front porch. On summer evenings they captured

Figure 5.1 At Georgia State College for Women, Mary Flannery (right) attended a three-year accelerated program, created so its graduates could fill the jobs of men who left to fight in World War II. She became art editor of the college newspaper, the *Colonnade*, and editor-in-chief of the *Corinthian* literary magazine.

lightning bugs and took turns on a swing hung from the massive branches of an ancient pecan tree in the front yard. In good weather, Mary Flannery went with the Cline girls to the family farm outside town to ride horses and play in the woods.

At Georgia College, Mary Flannery thought deeply about the books she read and the papers she wrote. She engaged her professors in intellectual conversations and academic arguments, starting in her freshman year with Professor Paul Boeson, who taught a literature survey course that covered Plato and Aristotle. Mary Flannery and Professor Boeson talked every day before class, another student said later.

In a freshman composition course, she spent most of every class arguing with the teacher, herself a writer but in the sort of nostalgic and romantic style that Mary Flannery disliked. Sparring verbally with teachers was a way for her to work out her ideas about literature and writing.

But a different composition professor, Hallie Smith, was so enthusiastic about Mary Flannery's writing that she gave her top grades, "A+" and "A!" At Professor Smith's suggestion, Mary Flannery submitted descriptive sketches composed for class to the *Corinthian*, the college literary magazine. Mary Flannery's writing showed that she had devoured difficult novels by newly acclaimed writers like James Joyce and William Faulkner. On the other hand, she dismissed much of the assigned poetry, in particular labeling the respected American poet Emily Dickinson as "froth."

In class discussions with her philosophy professor, George Beiswanger, Mary Flannery showed the wide range of her reading, back to the medieval religious philosopher Thomas Aquinas. Professor Beiswanger wrote that she was a "first-rate intellectual" and a "born writer."

But Mary Flannery didn't abandon cartooning. At Georgia College, one central idea, or "rabbit," for her was the desire of fellow students to escape college lectures and avoid doing homework. In one of Mary Flannery's cartoons, a girl who looks bored asks the librarian for books *not* recommended by a teacher.

In her prints, she began creating distinctive female characters, many with exaggerated or unusual features that gave clues to their personalities. In one cartoon, a nerdy-looking girl wears heavily black-rimmed

"Do you have any books the faculty
doesn't particularly recommend?"

"I understand she says it's
the happy way of doing things."

Figure 5.2 In cartoons, Mary Flannery portrayed students complaining or trying to avoid school work.

glasses as she sits on the sidelines at a party while everyone else is dancing enthusiastically. But she appears proud of her academic abilities, with her big smile and her words in the caption: "I can always get a Ph.D."

Two students who became Mary Flannery's favorite cartoon characters had especially long, awkwardly positioned feet, and they frowned, scowled, or looked disappointed as they talked about college life. The two often complained about the military women, shown in cartoons, who were marching around their college. (When Georgia College was selected to be a training center for the newly founded women's military corps known as the WAVES [Women Accepted for Voluntary Emergency Service], many students were unhappy about the invasion of their quiet campus.)

To sign her cartoons, Mary Flannery developed a pictogram, a drawing that conveys meaning the way a squiggly black line on a yellow road sign

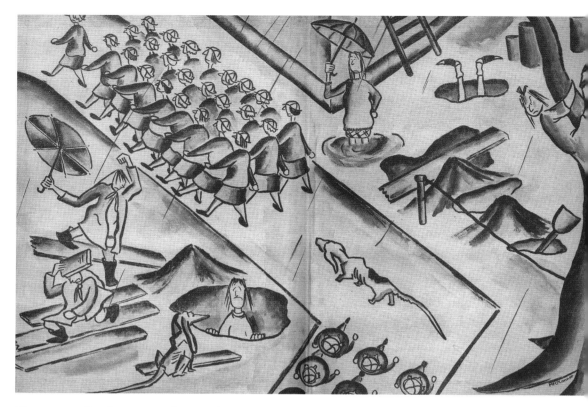

Figure 5.3 During Mary Flannery's years at Georgia College, students were unhappy that the newly founded women's military corps conducted training exercises on the otherwise peaceful green lawns of their campus.

warns of a curvy road ahead. She merged her initials to create the shape of a bird. Mary Flannery surrounded herself with birds throughout her life whenever she could, beginning with chickens, ducks, and geese but ending up with a much more unusual species, the peacock.

Mary Flannery's cartoons appeared in almost every issue of Georgia College's newspaper, the *Colonnade*, where she became the art editor. At the same time, she became editor-in-chief of the *Corinthian*, a literary magazine where she published short stories and humorous articles. Mary Flannery wrote a satirical review of the children's book *The Story of Ferdinand*, about a stubbornly peaceful bull, as well as an essay called "Why Worry the Horse" about a world in which people returned to horse transportation. She also wrote darker fiction like the Edgar Allan Poe stories she had liked most as a child.

Figure 5.4 As a cartoonist, Mary Flannery came up with an artful signature that combined her initials, MFOC, in the shape of something she loved: a bird.

Mary Flannery was still "physically . . . a bit awkward," according to Betty Boyd Love, a lifelong friend she met at college. Love wrote about Mary Flannery's dry, whimsical humor and said, "She knew who she was, and what she was, and was neither over-pleased nor disturbed by either." Other classmates said they liked Mary Flannery because she was so honest.

When one student told Mary Flannery that she wished she could borrow some of her creativity, Mary Flannery answered, "I'd exchange it for your ability to attract the men." The boy Mary Flannery had a crush on during college, John Sullivan, left Milledgeville to fight with the Marines in the Pacific and later trained to be a priest. But having a less-active social life could be an advantage, she said later: "Needing people badly and not getting them may turn you in a creative direction."

Mary Flannery purposely avoided acting more clever than the other students. Classmates remember a professor's asking students to name their favorite book, and most tried to sound impressive by choosing classics by famous authors like Charles Dickens. But Mary Flannery amused them by naming the Sears, Roebuck catalogue, the one store catalogue that many families received each year. Fat as an old-fashioned dictionary, the Sears catalogue sold everything from spoons and socks to washing machines, cars, and prefabricated houses.

Mary Flannery disliked anyone acting as if they were better than others. Her years of observation helped her see beneath people's surface appearances For her, cartooning as well as story writing started with real people and real situations, not abstract ideas such as a belief in goodness or God.

"Oh, well, I can always be a Ph.D."

Figure 5.5 The girl in the cartoon who is not dancing energetically pins her hopes on the academic success of earning a graduate degree. After she drew this, Mary Flannery entered a graduate program and became a respected intellectual and writer.

Flannery O'Connor on Connections between Seeing and Writing

Flannery believed that her years of cartooning gave her the visual skills combined with insight and humor that made her fiction come alive for readers. In lectures and essays, she directly linked vision to writing when she advised, "You've got to learn to paint with words."

Flannery showed that she knew well the common challenge to writers to "show don't tell" when she warned in her lectures, "Never go inside a character's head until you know what he looks like."

The challenge was one she repeated often, as when she said, "A story is . . . *not about telling* the reader something. A story is about *showing*. What the fiction writer had to learn was how to become a graphic artist."

For anyone who thought they might want to write fiction someday, she suggested, "Start reading and writing and *looking* and listening. Pay less attention to yourself than what is outside you."

And finally, she expanded the seeing-writing connection to include all five senses when she said, "Fiction operates through the senses. . . . The first and most obvious characteristic of fiction is that it deals with reality *through what can be seen*, heard, smelt, tasted and touched."

O'Connor, *Habit of Being*, 83; Magee, *Conversations with Flannery O'Connor*, 60; Burchby, "How Flannery O'Connor's Early Cartoons Influenced Her Later Writing"; Magee, *Conversations with Flannery O'Connor*, 17; O'Connor, *Mystery and Manners*, 91.

Every week, Mary Flannery sent cartoons to the *New Yorker*, a magazine of news, essays, short stories, and cartoons. Intellectual Americans have read the *New Yorker* since it was founded in February 1925, only about a month before Mary Flannery was born. When all her cartoons were rejected, she was disappointed but later acknowledged, "I just couldn't draw very well."

As graduation got closer, Professor Beiswanger suggested that Mary Flannery apply to the journalism program at the University of Iowa for a scholarship that paid full tuition plus $65 a term. She was excited about the chance to move away from Milledgeville and the South. When she received the scholarship, her relatives predicted that she would never last so far from home and said they expected her back in three weeks.

Mary Flannery would prove these naysayers very wrong, with her determination and with the creative talent that enabled her to turn her attention from cartooning to become a full-time fiction writer.

Part III

The Writing Life, 1945–1964

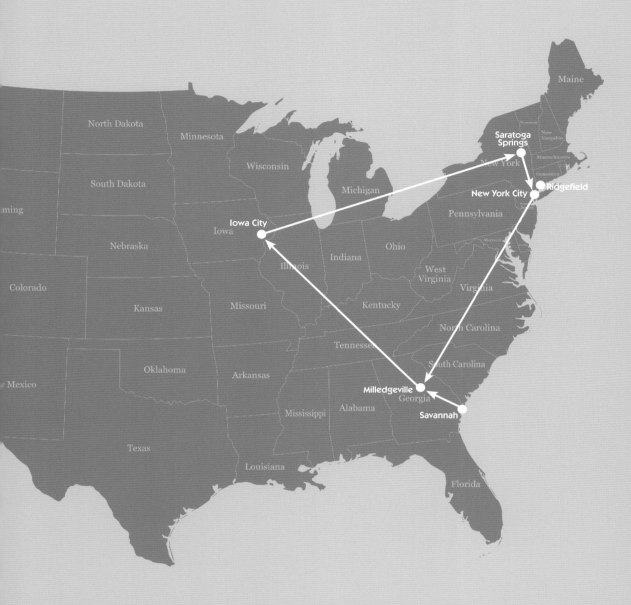

Figure 6.1 Mary Flannery left Georgia and the South, first to head west to Iowa for graduate school and then to head east to New York to write. In Iowa, she changed her name, dropping Mary and becoming Flannery O'Connor.

Chapter Six
Becoming a Writer

Mary Flannery headed west for her graduate journalism program, bringing with her a fifteen-pound muskrat fur coat. She hoped the fur would keep her warm during the long, cold Iowa winters. Regina accompanied her twenty-year-old daughter on the train and stayed in Iowa City long enough to help her get settled. During the five or so years Mary Flannery lived away from home, she wrote her mother a letter every day.

At the university, Mary Flannery's dorm room windows looked out onto expanses of flat farmland, thousands of acres extending in all directions. Like Milledgeville, Iowa City had a small downtown spread around the university with its wide green lawns. But buildings at the University of Iowa were massive and made of dark gray stone instead of Georgia College's red bricks with white-painted trim. Entirely unfamiliar to Mary Flannery were the biting cold winters when mountains of white snow buried everything in sight.

Almost right away, Mary Flannery made a discovery that may have upset her at first: she was "not a journalist," as she put it. That is, she was not interested in writing about daily news or about anything strictly factual, the kind of writing demanded by the journalism program she had just entered. Instead, she craved the freedom to imagine and create stories in her own voice and style. So she must have been ecstatic when she found, right down the street in Iowa City, the country's first and finest program in "imaginative writing," the Iowa Writers' Workshop.

With her mind made up, Mary Flannery crossed the campus to speak with Paul Engle, the program's director. When she explained her situation, Engle said later, he was mystified. In the story Engle told often, he handed

🢒 Genres: Different Kinds of Writing

Fiction comes from the imagination:

—fairy tales

—short stories

—novels

—graphic stories and novels

Non-fiction is based on facts, but often written with creativity:

—journalism: newspapers, magazines, internet news sites

—books: on history, science, and other topics

—autobiography and memoir: accounts of an author's own life

—biography: an account of one person's life written by someone else

—essays: a writer's thoughts and observations based on true stories or
    experiences, sometimes written creatively like fiction

---

her a pad of paper and a pencil and asked her to please write down what she wanted, because, he said, "I understood nothing, not one syllable."

Mary Flannery had arrived in a world far from the South, and here her rich Georgia drawl was incomprehensible. Once she wrote down her request and provided samples of her writing, including a few short stories that Engle called "imaginative, tough, alive," he immediately accepted her into the Workshop. She made the switch with no apparent disruptions in funding or lodging or any objections from Regina.

Signing on to become a fiction writer was the moment for a new name. About the name Mary Flannery, she later told a friend, "Who was likely to buy the stories of an Irish washerwoman?" When she chose Flannery O'Connor as her new name, some people thought she was honoring Cousin Katie Flannery Semmes, donor of her favorite childhood chickens.

At the Writers' Workshop, Flannery worked so hard at her writing that

Figure 6.2 When Mary Flannery entered the Iowa Writers' Workshop, the graduate writing program considered the best in the country, it was housed in small temporary structures that students called quonset huts.

she often ate breakfast and lunch in her bedroom. Distracting her from work was nearly impossible, one of her Iowa roommates said. While she kept up her reading of literary classics, Flannery spent long hours writing fiction as well as reading her classmates' work. She discovered how much she could learn from the way both students and teachers reacted to her writing.

"Writers are born," Flannery believed, "but they have to be nourished." Creative writing programs nourish young writers by giving them frequent opportunities to hear criticism of their own and one another's work. Because words mean different things to different people, even the most experienced and successful writers rely on others to read what they've written. They need to be sure the exact meaning they intend is getting across.

Competing against talented and more seasoned writers, Flannery had her first short story, "The Geranium," accepted for publication in a literary

— "The Geranium"

Getting her first short story published was a victory and a big step forward for Flannery. In the story "The Geranium," a homesick southerner living in New York City sits for hours staring out his back window. He longs for signs of home, maybe for some of the same things that Flannery missed, such as humid weather and Spanish moss, living so far from her native South.

> He looked over the paper at the window across the alley. The geranium wasn't there yet. . . . He didn't like flowers, but the geranium didn't look like a flower. It looked like the sick Grisby boy at home and it was the color of the drapes the old ladies had in the parlor.

O'Connor, "The Geranium," in *Collected Works*, 707.

magazine called *Accent*. She said later that she hadn't thought of herself as a true fiction writer until this small but well-regarded journal accepted her story.

While at Iowa, Flannery started the novel that she would continue to work on for almost six years. She developed a disciplined schedule of writing for several hours every day, even on Sundays. She reread what she had written and edited and rewritten, and then showed parts of the novel to her classmates. Based on their reactions and her evolving ideas about the book, she edited and rewrote some more.

During this process, she kept changing almost everything, including the title. First it was *The Great Spotted Bird*, then *Wise Blood and Simple*, and finally *Wise Blood*. The main character began as a homesick southern boy who, after repeated revisions, became a rebellious preacher called Hazel Motes. It took Flannery almost the entire six years to get a handle on Hazel's character.

At Iowa, Flannery also kept a journal of her prayers. She tried to stick to thanking God, but sometimes she couldn't resist asking God for a little help with her writing and then for a little more help getting that writing published. "I want so to love God all the way," she wrote. "At the same time I want all the things that seem opposed to it—I want to be a *fine* writer. Any success will tend to swell my head." One day she wrote, "Dear God, tonight it is not disappointing because you have given me a story."

In writing to God, Flannery described personal struggles that she probably shared with no one: "Dear God, I am so discouraged about my work. . . . Help me with this life that seems so treacherous, so disappointing." And she used her prayers to confess: "Dear God, In a way I got a good punishment for my lack of charity to Mr. Rothburg [a fellow student] last year. He came back at me today like a tornado . . . I say many many too many uncharitable things about people everyday. I say them because they make me look clever."

In her second year at Iowa, Flannery learned about an award given every year to a work of fiction by a Writers' Workshop student and worked hard to complete an early manuscript of *Wise Blood*. She won, a terrific stroke of good fortune for her that was the fruit of her talent and hours of hard work. As part of the award, the respected publisher Rinehart & Company would consider publishing Flannery's novel. Most first-time novelists struggle, sometimes for years, to have publishers agree even to look at their work. The award came with $750, which served as an "advance" payment, to be subtracted from profits earned once the book was published. (A young writer starting out today would be very happy to receive the current equivalent of more than $10,000.

Flannery was pleased with the publishing deal and the money, though she now felt under more pressure than ever to finish. "Writing a novel is a terrible experience," she wrote later, "during which the hair often falls out and the teeth decay. I'm always highly irritated by people who imply that writing fiction is an escape from reality." And Flannery once told students, "When I sit down to write, a monstrous reader looms up who sits down beside me and continually mutters, 'I don't get it, I don't see it, I don't want it.'"

Flannery O'Connor completed the Iowa Writers' Workshop at age twenty-two, young to have acquired a graduate degree. She traveled to

Georgia for the summer and then returned to Iowa for one more snowy year with a fellowship that paid her to teach writing. That fall, without the roommates she'd had in graduate school and far from home, Flannery was alone for the first time in her life. She had a small, simple room in a boardinghouse with a narrow twin bed and a desk for her typewriter, where she usually kept a package of vanilla wafer cookies to snack on while writing.

As that year was ending, Flannery was thrilled to learn she'd won a coveted spot at the "artists' colony" called Yaddo in upstate New York In the recommendation Paul Engle wrote for her, he called Flannery "one of the best young writers in the country."

As her taxi wound its way from the train station and uphill through dense pine trees to Yaddo, Flannery found herself in yet another unfamiliar part of the country, the Northeast. At Yaddo, she was grateful for the private living quarters, prepared meals, and a peaceful place to write surrounded by about forty acres of deep woods, wildlife, and extensive flower gardens.

With silence at Yaddo imposed every day from 9 a.m. to 4 p.m., Flannery continued to revise *Wise Blood*. In the evenings, she got to know other residents, mostly writers and a handful of painters and composers, although she did not join the wild, late-night parties.

Among those who became close friends, Flannery's favorite was the highly acclaimed poet Robert Lowell. "He is one of the people I love," she said later. Sometime afterward, Lowell mentioned that at Yaddo Flannery suffered from the undiagnosed pains that would soon become more serious.

Robert Lowell gave Flannery an important opportunity, a personal recommendation to a literary agent named Elizabeth McKee. Essential to successful writers, literary agents can help authors, first to find a publisher interested in their book, and then to deal with contracts and other business arrangements involved in the publishing process. Usually, young writers send their manuscripts to many agents before one agrees to take them on.

➤ Writing Retreats

For writers and artists, "retreats" can provide an escape from daily schedules and responsibilities—with no expenses or other people to worry about. Yaddo is one of the oldest writers' retreats in the United States and has a highly selective entry process. At Yaddo, daytime hours are spent working in solitude, while at night talented artists of all kinds get together to party, relax, and share ideas. After the retreat ends, friendships among writers often endure and offer support as well as useful contacts. Yaddo writers have won top literary awards, including the Nobel Prize for Literature, the Pulitzer Prize, and the National Book Award.

When she first wrote to Elizabeth McKee, Flannery didn't try to portray herself as accomplished or successful, as most writers would do. Instead, she wrote, "I am a very slow worker . . . let me know if you would like to look at what I can get together when I get it together." McKee read Flannery's work and right away accepted the young author and her still-incomplete novel.

Flannery's streak of successes seemed to be coming to an end when her editor at Rinehart, John Selby, sent her his criticisms of *Wise Blood*. Selby began by welcoming Flannery in a way that would make almost every young writer ecstatic. But then he called her novel unconventional and limited, meaning that the book would not make money. While Flannery knew most young writers would be eager to accept any suggestions from Selby, she was not.

What Selby criticized in *Wise Blood* was exactly what Flannery wanted in her book. She needed her characters to be unconventional and limited, to show that they were southerners and to show that they were "touched for better or worse by God." She wanted her characters unusual enough to get her readers' attention.

A novelist puts the meaning of life in a story by way of odd and specific details, Flannery explained, like her description of the grandfather in *Wise Blood* as "a waspish old man who had ridden over three counties with Jesus hidden in his head like a stinger."

Flannery told Elizabeth McKee that the thought of working with Selby and specifically of responding to his criticisms "is repulsive to me." She also refused Selby's request to send him a summary of her novel. "I don't choose to waste my time at it," she explained to Paul Engle in Iowa. "I don't write that way."

Flannery's answer to Selby was direct, bordering on rude: "I would not like at all to work with you as do other writers. . . . I am not writing a conventional novel, and I think the quality of the novel I write will derive precisely from the peculiarity or aloneness . . . of the experiences I write from."

By refusing to do what a respected editor asked, Flannery took an enormous risk that her writing might never get published. Although she was only twenty-four years old, she knew exactly what she wanted to do as a writer, even if it was taking her a while to get there. At this point, Flannery had one more stroke of good fortune when Robert Lowell, the poet she met at Yaddo, introduced her to the editor-in-chief of a different publisher, Harcourt, Brace & Company. That editor, Robert Giroux, offered her an advance of $1,500, twice as much as Rinehart had, for the rights to publish her manuscript. Now she had an editor who was truly enthusiastic about her book.

Later Giroux said about Flannery, "Good writers . . . who are going to be successful know what they want to do. I think she had a great deal more confidence than most." (In the end, *Wise Blood* was so unusual that even Giroux had a hard time convincing his employer to go ahead and publish it.)

Flannery received permission to stay at Yaddo for about nine months, longer than most other artists who spent time there. Afterward, she moved to New York City, which had inspired many writers over the centuries and seemed a natural place for her to continue writing. Despite the noise, the crowds, and the loneliness of a big city, she liked New York, but she found living there very expensive.

Robert Lowell took her to meet his friends, Sally and Robert Fitzgerald. Each was a writer and editor, and they lived just outside the city in Connecticut. They invited Flannery to stay in their garage apartment as a paying guest, at $65 a month plus one hour of babysitting every afternoon. The Fitzgeralds became Flannery's closest friends, advocates, supporters, and trusted critics, and she came to consider their family her adopted kin.

So far, on the path to becoming an acclaimed fiction writer, Flannery O'Connor had the kind of opportunities that would make any writer green with envy: attending the Iowa Writers' Workshop, residing at Yaddo, and gaining access to agents and publishers. These opportunities seemed almost to drop into her lap but were in fact the result of her enormous talent and blossoming abilities as a writer of exhilarating fiction. Still, the hard work of writing that fiction remained up to her, and she was about to encounter a challenge she could never conquer.

Figure 7.1 When Flannery became ill, Regina took over management of a working dairy farm with fifty cows so she could support her daughter's writing career.

Chapter Seven
Return to the South

For the Christmas before her twenty-fifth birthday, Flannery headed home to Georgia for the holidays. She'd been living with the Fitzgeralds in Connecticut when she began to suffer from muscle aches and fatigue. She felt "a heaviness" in her arms but thought it might be caused by re-typing her entire *Wise Blood* manuscript on a manual (not electric) type-writer, using keys that required pushing with some force.

Flannery looked like "a shriveled-up old woman" when she got off the train in Atlanta, her uncle said. Her mother and relatives took her to the hospital where she stayed, sick and exhausted, for several months. The doctors told Flannery she had arthritis, painful swelling in the joints that she called "AWTHRITUS . . . what leaves you always willing to sit down, lie down, lie flatter, etc."

From her hospital bed she rewrote once again, this time by hand, all two hundred or so pages of *Wise Blood*. She had decided that her main char-acter, Hazel Motes, would blind himself at the end of the book. Now she needed to prepare readers for the new ending by going back through the novel to leave clues, mostly symbolic, such as truths Motes refused to see.

While some say Flannery learned her actual diagnosis when she overheard her mother talking with doctors outside her room, her friend Sally Fitzgerald may have been the one who finally told her. Flannery did not have arthritis but lupus, the same disease that had killed her father about ten years earlier. Lupus can run in families, but that was not well understood at the time. By the early 1950s, a new class of drugs called steroids helped control the symptoms of lupus by suppressing the immune system to keep it from attacking the body's organs. When

Lupus

HOW: Antibodies that are produced by the body to fight viruses and other infections instead attack tissues in the bones, kidneys, heart, skin, blood cells, and nervous system.

WHO: Lupus affects nine times as many women as men, most often starting between ages fifteen and thirty-five.

COURSE: Lupus symptoms can flare up in episodes of fatigue, pain, and weakness, interspersed with remissions that are relatively symptom-free.

TODAY: After years of research and the discovery of new treatments, those with lupus are now often able to manage their disease and live a typical lifespan.

Flannery learned steroids were made using pigs' brains, she expressed her gratitude: "If pigs wore garments, I wouldn't be worthy to kiss the hems."

Flannery told people she had "red wolf," because *lupus* means wolf in Latin and the disease can cause a red rash across the nose that makes the face look like a wolf's bite. Flannery's lupus made her very tired and made her joints, especially her hips, stiff, swollen, and painful. Although steroids helped Flannery, a side effect was that they also weakened her bones, causing her to limp and eventually to need crutches.

For Flannery, lupus was "of no consequence to my writing, since for that I use my head and not my feet," she joked to friends. She rarely complained and sometimes saw the bright side of her condition: "when you can't be too active physically, there is nothing left to do but write so I may have a blessing in disguise."

Regina offered to care for her daughter in Milledgeville. Flannery had been leading a vibrant life as an independent and successful young woman, in the company of writers, and was opposed to living again in the South. Now, at only twenty-five years old, she was practically forced to move back to Georgia and back in with her mother.

Flannery said she had "stayed away from the time I was 20 until I was 25 with the notion that the life of my writing depended on my staying away." But to her surprise, she soon found, "The best of my writing has been done here."

Flannery believed that writing requires "a great deal of self-knowledge . . . to know yourself is to know your region . . . and the world." For her, that world was the South. Living in Milledgeville again gave her daily, firsthand experience of everything southern that she needed for her work, from characters and geography to the region's diverse accents. About the southern way of speaking, she believed that the sounds "build up a life of their own in your senses."

When the stairs in the Clines' Green Street house became too difficult for Flannery to manage, Regina moved them both to the nearby family farm, which Flannery renamed Andalusia. The modest old wooden farmhouse sat on a hillside up a dirt road from the single-lane highway leading out of Milledgeville. Rocking chairs on the screened-in front porch looked over a pond and woods of cypress and loblolly pines.

Although the farm was an inheritance, meaning the two paid nothing to live there, money was scarce and medical bills were high. At the age of fifty-six, Regina had never worked at all for a living, much less worked a five-hundred-acre farm. But she bought fifty dairy cows, hired a family to help out, and went into the milk business.

Regina took care of most of the practical arrangements of her daughter's life, leaving Flannery free to spend her often-limited energy on writing. "I don't know what I would do without her," Flannery told a friend about Regina. Although her mother never came around to liking Flannery's books, the dedication at the beginning of *Wise Blood* reads simply "For Regina."

On the first floor of the Andalusia farmhouse, Regina fixed up the front living room as Flannery's bedroom. Her typewriter sat on an old brown wooden desk next to a single bed. Flannery described the room as "a cross between a hospital and a monk's cell" but said she had everything she

Figure 7.2 At Andalusia, the family farm outside Milledgeville, Flannery had a manual typewriter right next to her bed and kept strict hours for writing every day in this room.

needed to live and write. She kept a pen and paper under her pillow for jotting down ideas that occurred to her in the night.

A great advantage of living at the farm was that Flannery could once again surround herself with her favorite birds. She accumulated pens of pheasants and quails, a flock of turkeys, more than a dozen geese, and a tribe of mallard ducks. Still, she felt "a lack," as she put it later.

Then, one day peacocks arrived on the train from Florida, two adult peafowl and four peachicks that she'd ordered through the mail. At the Milledgeville train station, "the crate was on the platform and from one end of it protruded a long, royal-blue neck and crested head," she wrote. "When I first uncrated those birds . . . I said, 'I want so many of them that every time I go out the door I'll run into one.'"

In her fiction, Flannery described some characters as peacock-like, strutting like a peacock, or acting as proud or sensitive as a peacock. She

Figure 7.3 Flannery owned birds through most of her life but felt "a lack" until mail-ordered peacocks arrived in crates at the train station. At Andalusia, the peacocks kept visitors awake at night with screams that sounded like "Help!"

believed the male peacock is vain about his beautiful plumage, showing it only when it pleases him to do so, but that his vanity is offset by ugly feet. Flannery may have shared some personal character traits with her peacocks: "odd, comic, proud, vain in spite of itself, resplendent in short bursts," observed one critic.

Sometimes as many as forty of these large, noisy birds wandered around the farm and perched in the trees at night, screaming, as Flannery said, "like hungry babies." When one visitor to the farm headed for bed, she warned him, "Don't be alarmed if you hear something that sounds like 'Help!' It's only the peacocks!"

In the mornings, while Flannery concentrated on her writing, Regina went to town on business and errands. By lunchtime, she was a gold mine of information and told her daughter whatever stories and gossip she'd picked up. When Flannery couldn't get around easily on her own, Regina

Figure 7.4 Living on the farm Andalusia, Flannery wrote for several hours every morning. Regina often did errands in town and afterward brought her daughter local gossip and stories.

made sure she never lacked for colorful details of local life. Flannery wrote, "It is a great blessing, perhaps the greatest blessing a writer can have, to find at home what others have to go elsewhere seeking."

Many of Flannery's friends and literary acquaintances made the long trek to visit her at Andalusia. Some complained that Regina talked so much they rarely got to hear Flannery speak. But by keeping up the conversation that way, Regina relieved her daughter from making too much effort, which might exhaust her and make her sicker.

Regardless of guests or anything else going on, Flannery kept to her disciplined writing schedule, spending two to three hours at her typewriter every morning. She was, as she put it, "a full-time believer in writing habits," because ideas were more likely to come when you were at your desk working. And when they do come, you should be sitting there at the ready. Talent "is simply something that has to be assisted all the time by physical and mental habits or it dries up and blows away," Flannery said.

Figure 7.5 *Wise Blood* upset Flannery's family and neighbors, who complained about shocking religious blasphemy and gritty descriptions of graffiti on the walls of men's bathrooms.

Figure 7.6 After six years and dozens of rewrites, *Wise Blood* came out in 1952, receiving mixed reviews at first but gaining acclaim in the years to come. Flannery spoke at book signings (seated) and lectured to students throughout the country.

"I rewrite, edit and throw away," she admitted. "Sometimes I work for months and have to throw everything away." One example of how much rewriting she did is preserved among her manuscripts in the Flannery O'Connor Collection at Georgia College: seventeen versions of one short scene that takes place on a porch.

Flannery continued to send drafts of her writing to friends and others, and she tried to listen openly to their advice and suggestions. Sally Fitzgerald praised Flannery's "willingness to learn [except for] how to spell."

Wise Blood was published in 1952. Over time it became successful and inspired an acclaimed feature-length film, but not all early reviews of the book were good. Flannery's Georgia friends and relatives were horrified by the gritty descriptions of graffiti on the walls of men's bathrooms and the religious blasphemy they found shocking. Milledgeville readers wondered whether the book's unpleasant characters revealed how Flannery viewed them, her friends and neighbors, in this small town.

Before she read the book, Flannery's cousin Katie Semmes bought many copies to send as gifts to her priest and members of the Savannah clergy. But when she finally had a chance to read it, Katie was so upset she sent apologies to everyone, and people said she went to bed for a week. Flannery wrote a friend about her "83-year-old cousin who was fond of me and I was convinced that my novel was going to give her a stroke . . . all I got was a curt note saying I do not like your book."

When she first began to write, Flannery worried about "this thing of scandalizing people." But to the question of whether she longed for her writing to be more popular, she answered, "I can wait. A few readers go a long way when they're the right kind." When one critic wrote that Flannery O'Connor's "picture of the modern world is terrifying," her publisher defended her, saying that negative reviewers "all recognized her power but missed her point."

Three years later, in 1955, Flannery had almost immediate success with the collection of her short stories titled *A Good Man Is Hard to Find* (also the name of the book's first story). The influential *New York Times Book Review* called her book "***revolutionary***" and compared Flannery's talent and passion in her writing to the passion of her religious beliefs. With

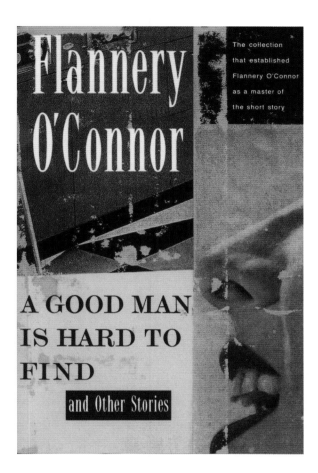

Flannery O'Connor

A GOOD MAN IS HARD TO FIND

and Other Stories

Figure 7.7 Flannery's book *A Good Man Is Hard to Find* includes a short story with the same title and the most famous of her characters, a criminal called The Misfit.

these stories, most critics agreed, Flannery O'Connor's talents began to flourish, as one masterpiece followed another.

Most of her short stories take place on farms or in remote rural settings in the American South. Many of the main characters are either poorly educated and narrow-minded or well-educated and pretentious. Most end up doing something foolish, thoughtless, or nasty with unfortunate results. Reviewers commented on Flannery O'Connor's ability to see through to the core of people, enabling her to make characters come alive for her readers. Flannery called this ability her "habit of being," the intense and constant effort she made not just to observe but to think hard about what people were doing and why.

Flannery knew when she still had work to do on a piece of writing: if she didn't enjoy reading it, it wasn't finished. "I admire my own work as much if not more than anybody else does," she acknowledged. "I read [my stories] over and over and laugh and laugh, then get embarrassed when I remember I was the one wrote them." Flannery found her stories so amusing that she had trouble reading them aloud before an audience.

The one exception was the story "A Good Man Is Hard to Find," about The Misfit and the grandmother, a story she considered so grim that she managed to read it in public without laughing. Flannery took on a different voice for each character, as if she knew them so well she could become them. Some listeners shivered with fear when they heard The Misfit speak in a deep, cold, and uncaring voice.

When a reader complained that one story left a bad taste in her mouth, Flannery wrote back, "You weren't supposed to eat it." And her story collection did not win over her fellow Georgians. Flannery slightly exaggerated their objections when she quipped that in Georgia "escaped criminals do not roam the roads exterminating families." She was referring to The Misfit and his gang of murderers in the story "A Good Man Is Hard to Find." The story collection of the same name, *A Good Man Is Hard to Find*, made the American Library Association's list of "most banned and/or challenged books" of the twentieth century.

Meanwhile, Flannery's Connecticut friends, the Fitzgeralds, stayed in touch by letter and regular visits to Andalusia, even as they added a new baby to their family almost every year. Flannery dedicated the story collection *A Good Man Is Hard to Find* to Robert and Sally Fitzgerald, saying, "If I dedicated it to any of my blood kin, they would think they had to go into hiding."

Every day Flannery wrote long, detailed, and usually funny letters to close friends as well as to almost anybody else who wrote to her, strangers and critics alike. One letter from a stranger led to correspondence lasting nine years. To this woman, whom Flannery called "A," she wrote several lengthy letters almost every month before the two met in person. In writing to "A" and to many respected religious and philosophical thinkers of her day, Flannery explored serious questions about God and human existence.

When asked why she didn't marry, Flannery said she had been in love many times but that once she understood the physical limitations of lupus, especially the terrible fatigue, she had to be selective about where to direct her energies. And by choosing to focus on writing, she avoided "entangling love relationships," as she called them.

With the collection *A Good Man Is Hard to Find*, Flannery O'Connor's writing received so many positive responses that she was invited to appear as the first guest on the new television show *Galley Proof*. The show was filmed live, and *New York Times* book editor Harvey Breit interviewed her as he chain-smoked cigarettes. While the cameras were running, Flannery responded to Breit as directly and almost as impolitely as she had to her first editor, John Selby. When Breit asked whether she would like to summarize her story for the television audience, she answered, "No, I certainly would not." Flannery thought each word in her fiction was essential for saying what she wanted to say. By refusing to summarize her ideas, she left the writing to speak for itself.

Sometime later a letter-writer asked her about the restrictions lupus placed on her life, such as the inability to travel much for pleasure. Flannery responded by saying how illness can at times be "a place more instructive than a long trip to Europe." But when her disease got her down, she described "a place where there's no company, where nobody can follow."

When she was feeling better, Flannery managed to travel around the United States, often on her own with invitations from colleges and universities to speak about her books. She wanted to make money so she could contribute to household expenses and, in particular, buy appliances for her mother such as a telephone and a new refrigerator that "spits the ice cubes at you." On the other hand, she offered to give many lectures for free. Flannery also won grants and awards for her writing, including a grant from the Ford Foundation of $8,000 (worth about $70,000 today).

In all she gave about sixty lectures, and she worked hard to make them interesting. At Emory University in Atlanta, a student described Flannery's talk as "the hit of the season."

In both lectures and letters, she gave generous advice to young writers. "How do you write a novel?" one student asked. "Do you outline?" Flannery replied that she didn't, that instead "I just kind of feel it out like a hound-dog. I follow the scent. You know the direction you're going in, but you don't know how you'll get there."

In 1960, Flannery published her second novel, *The Violent Bear It Away*, with the main character a teenager named Tarwater, who is both a pyromaniac and a prophet. While many praised the novel, some readers thought it included too many religious fanatics.

In November 1963, Flannery had surgery related to her lupus. Afterward, she was too weak to type or even to attend Mass. She became enthusiastic about TV and that same month watched what she called the "sad news" about the assassination of John F. Kennedy, who had been especially important to her as America's first Catholic president.

Flannery remained in the Atlanta hospital for months, her face puffy and her eyelids swollen nearly shut. From her hospital bed, she worked on her second short story collection, writing mostly by hand and then in rare spurts of energy using an electric typewriter to keep rewriting and editing. Published in 1965 after her death, the collection is named for its title story, "Everything That Rises Must Converge," the story of two women, one white and one Black, wearing identical hats and riding a city bus with their sons, which reflects the growing racial tensions of the 1960s. After the characters get off the bus, the white woman tries to give a "bright new penny" to the Black woman's son, a gesture that further fuels the anger that has been building in his mother until she swings her large red purse and knocks the other woman down.

Still in the hospital the following spring, in 1964, Flannery joked that she was "hearing the celestial chorus," as if she were in heaven, but the song in her head was the American folk song "Clementine." In late July, Flannery became so ill that she slipped into a coma. She died on August 3, 1964, at age thirty-nine. Though her lupus had been diagnosed almost fifteen years earlier, no one expected her to die so young.

Mary Flannery O'Connor was buried in Memory Hill Cemetery in Milledgeville next to her father in the red clay earth of the Georgia she

Flannery O'Connor's Advice to Writers

In her lectures, Flannery offered clues to her own success as a writer, including attitudes and practices that began in her childhood, such as, "The writer is only free when he can tell the reader to go jump in the lake." She joked with young writers about how "you always have to work in a room where you're alone. If you're in a place where there are only two rooms, get everybody else in that other room." She warned them that writers pay attention to "what we don't understand rather than what we do." And she addressed the biggest challenge for most fiction writers—how to create characters who come alive on the page—by advising that "the serious writer has always taken the flaw in human nature for his starting point, usually the flaw in an otherwise admirable character."

Magee, *Conversations with Flannery O'Connor*, 39; Gentry and Amason, *At Home with Flannery O'Connor*, 73; O'Connor, "Some Aspects of the Grotesque in Southern Fiction," in *Mystery and Manners*, 42; O'Connor, "Novelist and Believer," in *Mystery and Manners*, 167.

had come to cherish. Regina O'Connor lived to be ninety-nine years old, dying in 1995, more than thirty years after her daughter.

Near the end of her life, Flannery sounded as if she was aware of how very sick she was and even that her death might be near when she said, "I've been writing eighteen years and I've reached the point where I can't do again what I know I can do well." She had done that writing so well that her most admired short stories and novels, as well as letters and essays, would be read long after her death.

Epilogue

Time magazine in 1965 called Flannery O'Connor a "verbal magician whose phrases flamed like matches in the dark." Her *Collected Works*, published in 1988 by the Library of America, became one of the best-selling titles in its collections by well-known American authors. For no twentieth-century author besides Flannery O'Connor was the growth in literary reputation after death so rapid or dramatic.

The rock band U2 paid tribute to Flannery at the 1987 Grammy music awards. The musician Bruce Springsteen in 2014 said about Flannery's short stories that they "landed hard on me . . . made me feel fortunate to sit at the center of this swirling black puzzle, stars reeling overhead, the earth barely beneath us."

In addition to the film of *Wise Blood*, six of Flannery O'Connor's short stories were filmed for TV, with "The Displaced Person" shot at Andalusia. Two documentary films explored her life and legacy.

In 2015, Flannery O'Connor's portrait graced a U.S. postage stamp in the Literary Arts series, chosen among more than thirty thousand suggestions from the public. Fans of Flannery O'Connor founded societies outside the United States, with the largest and most passionate group of followers in Japan. A huge growth in overseas sales came after one of her books was translated into Mandarin Chinese.

Over time, readers of Flannery's fiction drew attention to the racist language in letters she wrote to friends and family. Two well-known African American artists who lived near Milledgeville during Flannery's years there commented on the issue. The writer Alice Walker said about a letter of Flannery's, "one assumes she made this [racist] comment in an attempt at levity. Even so, I do not find it funny." Concerning Flannery's fiction, Walker added, "She also cast spells and worked magic with the written word. The magic, the wit, and the mystery of Flannery O'Connor I know I will always love." The painter Benny

Figure 8.1 In 2015, Flannery received the honor of a U.S. Postal Service stamp with her portrait and feathers of her much-loved bird, the peacock. Portrait by Sam Weber

Figure 8.2 *The Complete Stories* by Flannery O'Connor won the National Book Award in 1972 and after an online vote in 2009 was named the favorite award winner of the past sixty years.

Andrews wrote that Flannery O'Connor "depicted things bigger than the physical world she lived in. Nevertheless, she also retained a lot of the very worst . . . the society that she lived in was sustained by cruelty, oppression, and murder." Andrews said also that Flannery "confronts the leaping flames and churning waters. I've looked into her works, and I have found revelations." These remarks criticize the racism in Flannery's personal writing but praise her fiction.

➤ Voice in Fiction

Voice is the sound readers hear in a piece of writing—something every writer seeks but often has trouble creating. Readers recognize voice when they hear it, although it can be difficult to describe. For some authors, voice comes from the phrasing, accents, and vocabulary of a specific geographical region or period of history. For others, word choice suggests beliefs and attitudes. In Flannery's case, epigrams, or clever quotes—featured on postcards and displayed in houses where she lived as well as throughout the Flannery O'Connor Collection at Georgia College—show her gift for putting complicated thoughts into memorable words.

> "Bad children are harder to endure than good ones, but they are easier to read about," from "A Memoir of Mary Ann."

> "Nobody with a good car needs to be justified," from *Wise Blood*.

> "She would have been a good woman," said The Misfit, "if it had been somebody there to shoot her every minute of her life," from "A Good Man Is Hard to Find."

> "When in Rome, do as you done in Milledgeville," from a letter to a friend.

O'Connor, introduction to "A Memoir of Mary Ann," in *Flannery O'Connor: Collected Works*, 827; O'Connor, *Wise Blood*, 113; O'Connor, "Good Man," in *Complete Stories*, 133, O'Connor, *The Habit of Being*, 220.

When *The Complete Stories* by Flannery O'Connor won the National Book Award in 1972, it was the first time the judges unanimously decided to ignore the rule that prevented them from selecting the work of a writer who had been dead for more than two years. In 2009, the judges were proved right when ten thousand people voted online for their favorite National Book Award winner of the past sixty years. The winner: *The Complete Stories* by Flannery O'Connor.

Microsoft OneDrive is another cloud-based set of tools that lets you share your work with others. It is popular with businesses and older students. OneDrive includes many of the same features as G Suite. It has Word for word processing, Excel for spreadsheets, and PowerPoint for slide shows.

CHAPTER TWO

Share Settings

Once you have an account on a document sharing site, it's time to start creating work. When you log into G Suite or Microsoft OneDrive, you will see a list of your past documents. Here, you can search for and organize your files. From here, you can start a new project. You will begin by choosing the app you need to create your document.

Next, think about how you're **collaborating** with the person you'll be sharing the document with. Do you need to write an essay and then share it with someone who will edit it? Is this a project that you and a partner will work on together? Will you be dividing up the work? If so, you might share a blank document so that everyone starts the project at the same time.

What sharing rights should you give other people? It depends!

When you decide it's time to share, the next steps are pretty simple. You will share the document with only those who really need to see or use it. Click on the Share button in your document. If you're on your computer, this button is located at the top right of the screen in both G Suite and OneDrive. Type in your partners' email addresses, select your share settings, and send. Your partners will receive an email that gives them a link to the document.

You can choose to share as much or as little as you want. You can create documents and folders that are entirely private for you. Maybe you choose to share specific projects. Or you can choose to share an entire folder.

Try this:

In Google Drive, you have three options when you share a document:

1. **Edit:** Other people can make changes to your project. Anything you can do, they can do too!

2. **Comment:** Other people can look at your project and add notes or suggestions. These are not permanent changes to the document until you approve them.

3. **View:** Other people can look at your project. But they can't make changes or leave notes.

How do you know which sharing option to use? Think about each of the options above. When would you let someone edit your document? When would you only let them comment? When would you only let them view the document? Brainstorm some examples.

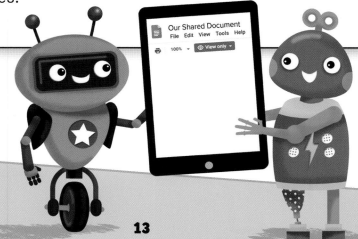

CHAPTER THREE

Communicate and Collaborate

Once you and your partners can access the document, it's time to collaborate! Collaboration is when you are all working together to create something.

Many people can work on a shared document at the same time. You'll be able to see who else has it open. Have you noticed the line that blinks right where you are about to type in a document? That's called the cursor. Everybody working on your document will have their own cursor. The cursors let you see where in the document your partners are working. Many partners find that it's best to work in different parts of the document. That way, you don't interrupt anyone's work.

You don't have to be in the same room to collaborate!

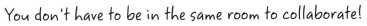

Collaboration involves a lot of communication. Are you working in the same room as your partners and not sharing a project online? If so, be sure to talk with them about where you are in the document. Tell them what your plans are. You can ask them questions and share ideas.

If you are not in the same room, you can communicate with tech tools! Use the Chat feature to talk to your partners without typing onto your project. Open up a chat and tell them your ideas and questions. Tired of typing? Use Google Hangouts or Skype instead. You can video chat while working on the project together. Remember, respect and kindness are always important when you are working in a group.

Decide on a plan at the beginning of your project. Your plan will help your project go smoothly.

16

Try this:

The best groups set "norms," or rules, for working together on a project. Decide with your group how you will collaborate. Make sure everyone does an equal amount of work. Try to answer these questions together before you get started:

- What strengths does each member bring to the group? How will they teach or share those skills with others?
- What is everyone's role?
- What are your group's rules for communicating?
- How will you communicate if you have a question, concern, or problem?
- When does your group need to have each part of the project finished?
- How will you handle editing and proofreading for your project?

CHAPTER FOUR

Special Features for Sharing

You've created a document and shared it with others. You've set up rules for working in a group. What's next? The work! Here are some tricks and tips to make the most of your shared document.

Many groups have one person go on a computer to start the project and set up a template. The template is like an outline that shows your group how the project will be **formatted**. It shows what questions need to be answered and where to type in your parts. Sometimes groups will set up a template together in person, with one person "driving" the computer. Then, groups can divide up and decide who will work on what. Templates can keep all team members more organized.

Do you ever "undo" or "redo" in a document? These are usually very helpful features. But they can make a mess in a shared document! If you press undo in a shared doc, the app will undo the last thing done to the document. But it might undo your partner's work instead of your own! Only use the undo and redo buttons if you are sure that you're the only person working on the document at that moment.

Some groups like to keep track of the work each person does on a project. Color coding makes it easy to see who created different parts. Each member of your group can choose to type in a different **font** color or style.

What happens if something gets deleted by mistake? What if you try out a new template but want to go back to the old one? There are many reasons that you may want to look at the Version History of your document. This feature will show you all of the earlier versions of the document. You will even be able to see who made different changes.

Sometimes we want to edit a document but don't want to change the original. This is a good time to Make a Copy of the project. After you've made a copy, it is automatically saved into your drive. Now you can edit the copy, but the original won't be changed.

Try this:

There are many special features included in the G Suite tools. The best way to learn about them is to use them! Try making a slide show with a friend about your favorite animals or video games. Make a birthday wish list and share it with your family members. Create a budget for your allowance. Then share it with your parents to show how responsible you are with your money. What will you do with a shared doc?

Color coding can help you see who is working on different parts of the project.

GLOSSARY

apps (APS) computer programs that perform special functions

cloud (KLOWD) space on the internet for storing information from your computer

collaborating (kuh-LAB-uh-rate-ing) working with others

data (DAY-tuh) information collected

drive (DRIVE) online storage that's used to save projects

essays (ES-ayz) short pieces of writing on a certain subject

font (FAHNT) style of printed letters and numbers

formatted (FOR-mat-ed) adjusted the appearance, shape, or style of something

spreadsheets (SPRED-sheets) computer programs that allow you to keep track of and use information related to numbers

surveys (sur-VAYZ) studies of the opinions or experiences of a group of people, based on their responses to questions

word processing (WURD PRAH-ses-ing) a system that allows people to create documents

BOOKS

Lovett, Amber. *Being a Team Player Online*. Ann Arbor, MI: Cherry Lake Publishing, 2020.

Reeves, Diane Lindsey. *Making Choices on My Team*. Ann Arbor, MI: Cherry Lake Publishing, 2018.

WEBSITES

Google Docs
https://www.google.com/docs/about
Create and collaborate using Google Docs.

Google Docs for Kids – Episode 1: What Is It?
https://youtu.be/478TDzL1b3E
Learn more about how to use Google Docs.

INDEX

About the AUTHOR

Ann Truesdell is a school librarian in Michigan. She and her husband, Mike, are the proud parents of James, Charlotte, Matilda, and Alice. They all enjoy reading, traveling, being outside, and spending time with their dog, Leia.